The American Civil War at Home

THE AMERICAN CIVIL WAR AT HOME

Edited by Scott Reynolds Nelson *and* Carol Sheriff

Virginia Sesquicentennial of the American Civil War Commission
Richmond, Virginia

©2014 by the
Virginia Sesquicentennial of
the American Civil War Commission

All rights reserved. First edition, published 2014.
Printed in the United States of America on acid-free paper.

ISBN 978-0-615-90592-1

The fifth in a series of seven Signature Conferences sponsored by the
Virginia Sesquicentennial of the American Civil War Commission,
"The American Civil War at Home" was held
April 20, 2013
at the College of William & Mary.

Library of Congress Control Number: 2013953339

Virginia Sesquicentennial of the American Civil War Commission
Richmond, Virginia

www.VirginiaCivilWar.org

Contents

Acknowledgments	vii
Preface	ix

Keynote Address   1

Lincoln, Slavery, and Emancipation
Eric Foner

Panel I: Emancipation and its Limits

The Shape of Freedom   15
Edward L. Ayers

Enslaved Women and the Battle for Freedom   21
and Democracy on the Civil War's Home Front
Thavolia Glymph

More Than Freedom: Black Northerners and the   27
Meaning of the Civil War
Stephen Kantrowitz

Panel I Discussion   35

Panel II: Internal Dissent in the Confederacy and the Union

Confederate Reckoning: The People And Their   48
Politics On The Homefront
Stephanie McCurry

The Other Emancipation: Plain Folk vs. Aristocrats   54
in the Invaded South
Stephen V. Ash

What Did Good Citizenship Mean during the Civil War? 62
J. Matthew Gallman

Panel II Discussion 71

PANEL III: QUESTION AND ANSWER SESSION 82

Contributors 101

Appendix: Further Reading 105

Index 108

Acknowledgments

Early in its work, the Virginia Sesquicentennial of the American Civil War Commission envisioned a series of annual conferences that would examine different aspects of the Civil War—from its causes, to military strategies and leadership in the North and South, to the key role of race and slavery in the conflict. That early idea has become the very popular Signature Conference series, which is presented in partnership with universities across the state, features the nation's finest historians, and hosts audiences of thousands. The 2013 Signature Conference, the fifth of seven, focused on the Civil War home front and the overwhelming social and political forces that forever changed Virginia and the nation 150 years ago.

Much of the success of the 2013 Signature Conference is due to the unwavering support of William and Mary president W. Taylor Reveley III. Special recognition extends to the host committee and key leaders, including Michael Fox, Jim Whittenburg, Melvin Patrick Ely, Scott Nelson, Carol Sheriff, Betty Flanigan, and Jodi Allen. In addition, the Choir of William and Mary performed a lively concert of Civil War songs, under the capable leadership of Dr. James Armstrong. Support of the Williamsburg community underpinned the conference, and special thanks go to the Colonial Williamsburg Foundation, Greater Williamsburg Chamber and Tourism Alliance, city manager Jack Tuttle, and Kate Hoving.

The Commission gratefully acknowledges the support of History, the Virginia Foundation for the Humanities, and many donors whose generosity made the 2013 Signature Conference possible.

At the start of the 2013 Signature Conference, the Commission was pleased to present its Distinguished Service Award to Dr. Charles F. Bryan, Jr., the driving force behind the creation of the Commission. Years before most of us knew how to pronounce "sesquicentennial," Charlie Bryan recognized the tremendous opportunities that it held, both as an education experience as well as a boon for travel and tourism. In early 2006, Dr. Bryan, who at the time was the President and CEO of the Virginia Historical Society, approached me about sponsoring legislation to establish the Virginia Sesquicentennial of the American Civil War Commission. From the beginning, he envisioned a commemoration that would be meaningful to all Americans today, understanding that history belongs to all of us. Without hesitation I can say that Dr. Bryan's leadership inspired many of the successful programs that are in place today.

Finally, the Commission deeply appreciates the tireless dedication and hard work of its staff, led with skill by executive director Cheryl Jackson. Many people ensured that the conference ran smoothly, and special recognition is due to a number of staff members and volunteers: Michele Howell, Kathleen DuVall, Scott Maddrea, Jeff Finch, Barbara Teague, Christine McCormick, Rusty Nix, Noelle Baker, Bill Ross, Chris Hairston, Dick and Rebecca Hickman, and Maggie and Andy Jackson. The delicate work of shaping the conference proceedings into a cohesive book was undertaken with care by Alexander Hartle. It is our hope that this work, like the conference series from which it was born, will endure for generations to come.

William J. Howell, Chairman
Virginia Sesquicentennial of the American Civil War Commission

Preface: The American Civil War at Home

Scott Reynolds Nelson

The Civil War is all around us, its vestiges in the most unlikely places. The war appears in everyday speech when we talk about privation with words like shoddy, greenback, poke salad, and tar heels. All these phrases suggest the wartime substitution of a cheap object for a better one: rags for wool, green dye for gold, pokeweeds for lettuce, and tar for shoe leather. This conference was not about the memorable battles, but about the war below the surface of events—the social conflict that still remains a century and a half after the shooting stopped. It brought together the historians who are most noted for exploring the social rifts that animated the war, the controversies engendered by it, and the ways in which, by 1863, a war *on* farms and homesteads became a war *in* farms and homesteads.

The very depth of this 150-year-old conflict has made memorializing difficult. The US Congress in the twenty-first century, perhaps wary of exacerbating sectional and ideological divisions, let die in committee efforts to establish a federal commission to commemorate the 150th anniversary of the Civil War. It is no small irony that Richmond, capital of the extinct Confederacy, would see more partisan harmony. The Virginia Sesquicentennial of the American Civil War Commission made it possible to bring an international collection of historians together to reconsider the Civil War. To commemorate the year that slavery ended, Carol Sheriff and I, along with Melvin Patrick Ely and

James Whittenburg, were given a free hand to choose whom to invite and the theme to consider. We decided upon "the American Civil War at Home."

Eric Foner began the conference with a keynote address that highlighted why 2013 was a particularly fitting year to commemorate the Civil War's influence on the domestic conflict. In *The Fiery Trial: Abraham Lincoln and American Slavery*, his path-breaking and prize-winning biography of Abraham Lincoln, Foner shows us how Lincoln's Emancipation Proclamation grew out of the war itself. Drawing on that larger work for his essay in this volume, Foner shows that Lincoln was antislavery, but no abolitionist. Like many of his generation, the sixteenth president simultaneously hated slavery and loved the Constitution. Thus he and many others faced a dilemma: the Constitution protected slavery. Lincoln sought to resolve this quandary with some constitutional form of emancipation. As Lincoln saw it, this meant compensating slaveholders for giving up their slave property. Since he regarded racism as unfixable, he sought to send freed slaves to live in colonies in Africa or the Caribbean.

But by 1863 the conflict had changed these traditional forms of reckoning. Foner notes four factors that influenced Lincoln to emancipate: a military stalemate on the battlefield, an antislavery Britain that might support the Confederacy if the war was not about slavery, the disintegration of slavery in areas around the fighting, and the decline of white enlistment in the North. Thus a combination of military and foreign policy, as well as social factors, pushed Lincoln to act as he did. Lincoln's military and foreign policy challenges by 1863 are well-known. What Foner shows is that the social conflict at home also altered the war's aims. He tells us that "slaves, ignoring Lincoln's insistence that the struggle was about national unity, began to seek refuge behind Union lines." As slavery crumbled on farms and homesteads, it shattered the decades-long tension between support for the Constitution and opposition to slavery. "War," he explains, "destabilizes slavery; it strips away its constitutional protections." With constitutional protection of slavery stripped away, Lincoln could make the bold move of declaring slavery ended and calling on former slaves to fill the ranks of the Union army and navy (thus fixing his recruitment problem, too). By war's end, two hundred thousand black men had done so. Once black men, free as well as formerly enslaved, fought for the Union, they were entitled, in Lincoln's view, to "a political voice in the reunited nation," Foner writes.

Three presentations, organized under the covering title "Emancipation and its Limits," immediately followed Foner's. Edward Ayers opens the panel with a closer view of emancipation and social conflict. He speaks about the *Visualizing Emancipation* website he is building with Scott Nesbit and others at the University of Richmond. "This is what the end of slavery looks like," he tells us, as attendees at the conference saw a multitude of red dots appear on a map of the American South in 1861. "Three weeks after Virginia secedes," he notes, "African Americans begin making themselves free." The home front, he shows, was in many places in the South all at once. "The home front is where there is an army eating your food" or where "there is an army taking away your livestock." He points out, too, that some parts of the South, such as the area around Appomattox, were "barely touched by the war," leaving slavery "barely disrupted." Factors that influenced home-front experiences include not just one's race but also one's age and family status, the area where Union troops came from, and the relative power of the Confederate army in the region. Ayers tells us that while many slaves escaped into Union lines in areas like Hampton, by the end of the war 3.5 million slaves did "not come into contact with the United States army." In this sense, he argues, the Thirteenth Amendment was not just a recognition that slavery had ended; it also made manifest the end of slavery that the Emancipation Proclamation only proposed.

Thavolia Glymph next calls our attention to the humanitarian crisis created by the war, particularly for the enslaved women and children who crossed into Union lines. Here the story is not of the Union valiantly assisting escaped slaves, but of "inept or uninterested federal commanders and soldiers" who created "'contraband' policies that varied from one command to the next." She asks that we consider enslaved women and children as the "unrecognized refugees" of the Civil War. (She borrows the term from modern studies of refugees elsewhere.) Why unrecognized? Relief agencies during the Civil War had important blind spots. When they wrote about "Union refugees," she explains, they were actually talking about white southern refugees who refused to support the Confederacy. Black refugees, by comparison, were hardly considered. Their claims to the rights of citizens were "debated" but seldom "recognized." Our understanding of their sacrifices during war and reconstruction has barely begun.

Finally Stephen Kantrowitz asks us to consider the abolitionists whom Lincoln knew about but failed to join with until late in the war. He gives us the story of the black abolitionists of Boston who had built, through protest and coalition politics, a political culture that wedded equality to freedom. It was this political culture that Lincoln finally recognized in the last days of his life—that African Americans were entitled not just to the fruits of their labor, but also to social and political equality. Or, as Kantrowitz puts it, "even the old colonizationist Abraham Lincoln had been won over to the idea that black soldiers represented not only a force against the Confederacy and slavery but an embodiment of the principles for which he wanted the reconstituted nation to stand." That ideal of the United States as a non-racial democracy, first articulated by free black Northern activists much earlier in the nation's history, and then absorbed by Lincoln in 1863 and 1864, finally became central to the meaning of the war itself.

All three of these presentations help us to understand that emancipation was not a top-down operation orchestrated by a Great Liberator, that it was incomplete in many parts of the nation, and that refugees—many of them women and children—made terrible and unacknowledged sacrifices. In this sense, emancipation 150 years ago was uneven and unexpected, yet it required a broad political movement that abolitionists had, in Foner's words, "staked out" decades earlier.

If the first session asked us to think more deeply about emancipation, the second panel asked us to think more carefully about what a "civil war" actually means. Dissent on the home front marked both the Union and Confederacy, yet with quite different valences and ranges of experience.

Stephanie McCurry begins by asking a very simple question: what was the Confederacy about? As she shows in her book, *Confederate Reckoning: Power and Politics in the Civil War South*, the Confederacy's origins rested on a small elite who pushed secession through with only 1.5 million of its 10 million people (that is, with only the white, male voting population) capable of choosing secession. With 85 percent of adult white men drawn into military service, white women—many from non-slaveholding families—pushed back against this nation-in-the-making. Through heartfelt and angry letters to Confederate governors and city riots over bread, they forced the Confederacy to reckon with its own undemocratic structure. To cope with these uprisings, the Confederacy was then forced to allocate critical supplies to the home front. In this way, McCurry argues, the failure of the Confederacy was as much political as military, as the conflict on the home front hobbled the Confederacy's ability to wage war.

Stephen Ash also seeks to understand the upheavals engendered by war. He notes that as Union forces moved into Nashville, New Orleans, Savannah, and Mobile, poor whites rioted, hindering Confederate attempts to maintain control of the cities as they tried to evacuate. When Union troops seized these towns, hundreds of white Southerners came to their aid, and tens of thousands of these white Southerners enlisted in Union army regiments. Other poor whites took advantage of the chaos of war to seize plantations and farms like the resort town of Beersheba Springs in Tennessee. But a widespread poor-white insurgency was stymied by three factors: racism among poor whites, the class prejudice of Union officers, and the vicious counteroffensive by elites after the war, a counteroffensive aided by Andrew Johnson's lenient policy toward former slaveholders. Ash encourages us to look past April 1865 when we try to characterize the home-front conflicts of the Civil War.

Finally, Matthew Gallman reconsiders the simplistic division between Copperheads (opponents of the war) and Unionists in the North. In comparison to the Confederacy, the Union drew a much smaller percentage of potential recruits into its ranks. Few Northerners faced the stark choices imposed by occupation, destruction, and the end of slavery. With more distance from the conflict, Northerners could think through the shades of gray between full-scale support for the war and outright opposition to it. Literary magazines sought to outline the difference between patriotic and unpatriotic behavior for those disengaged from the direct fighting, offering a wide range of deeds that could qualify as "patriotic." The home front in the Union was a different place, more a land of "shoddy" than of poke salad, giving citizens the freedom to take a range of positions on the conduct of the war.

All of these presentations demonstrate how vital the home front was to the war's progress. From abolitionism's political beginnings in the coalition politics of the North to the ways in which occupation unsettled slavery in areas close to the fighting, the home front was not a sideshow. It was where the war began and it changed the nature of the conflict. As Lincoln recognized the ways that social conflicts both limited and expanded his options, he embraced abolition, though the groundwork had been laid before he took pen to paper. Even once he declared slavery dead in those areas of the South still under rebellion, emancipation did not become a clear-cut story of slaves boldly seizing their freedom. Dangerous and even deadly consequences could await those slaves, women and children in particular, who sought safety behind Union lines, especially as places that fell under Union control one day could return to Confederate control the next. The military collapse of the Confederacy, too, involved more than soldiers, positions, and supply lines. The Confederate government proved incapable of creating a state that could support not only an army but also soldiers' families at home, and soldiers' wives continually demanded what they considered their due.

Yet as destabilizing as the war was for American society, the home front was not utter chaos, nor did its wartime disorder portend a full social upheaval at war's end. The war's revolutionary potential was dampened by the racial prejudice of poor white Southerners and the sudden return to power of the old elites in 1865—a re-ascendency that many white Northerners would themselves, in time, accept. This acceptance reflected Northerners' own ambivalence about whether emancipation should be accompanied by the full racial equality for which black abolitionists had long fought. The war's home front battles continued, albeit in different forms, well beyond the Confederacy's military surrender. Indeed the war's aftershocks may still be felt in everyday conflicts 150 years later as Americans still debate freedoms, the rights of citizens, and lessons of the war itself.

Lincoln, Slavery, and Emancipation

Eric Foner

Abraham Lincoln is the most iconic figure in American history. He exerts a unique hold on our historical imagination, as an embodiment of core American ideals and myths—the self-made man, the frontier hero, the liberator of the slaves. Thousands of works have been written about Lincoln, and almost any Lincoln you want can be found somewhere in the literature. He has been portrayed as a shrewd political operator driven by ambition, a moralist for whom emancipation was the logical conclusion of a lifetime hatred of slavery, and a racist who actually defended and tried to protect slavery. Politicians from conservatives to communists, civil rights activists to segregationists, have claimed him as their own.

Like all great historical transformations, emancipation during the Civil War was a process, not a single event. It played out over time, arose from many causes, and was the work of many individuals. It began at the war's outset when slaves, ignoring Lincoln's insistence that the struggle was about national unity, began to seek refuge behind Union lines. It did not end until December 1865, with the ratification of the Thirteenth Amendment irrevocably abolishing slavery throughout the reunited nation. But the Emancipation Proclamation was certainly the crucial step in this process.

In approaching the subject of Lincoln's views and policies regarding slavery and race, the first thing to bear in mind, as I emphasized in my recent book, *The Fiery Trial: Abraham Lincoln and American Slavery*, is that it is fruitless to identify a single quotation, speech, or letter, as the real or quintessential Lincoln. At the time of his death, Lincoln occupied a very different place with regard to these issues of slavery and race than earlier in his life. That Lincoln changed, of course, is hardly a new idea. But I try to tell the story, as it were, forward, not backward—not as a trajectory toward a predetermined goal, but as an unpredictable progress, with twists and turns along the way, and the future always unknown.[1]

I am particularly interested in Lincoln's relationship with abolitionists and with Radical Republicans, who in effect represented the abolitionist point of view in party politics. They often criticized him, and he made some unflattering remarks about them. Lincoln was not an abolitionist and never claimed to be one. Yet he saw himself as part of a broad antislavery movement that included both abolitionists and more moderate politicians of his own mold. He was well aware of the abolitionists' significance in creating public sentiment hostile to slavery. And on issue after issue—abolition in the nation's capital, wartime emancipation, enlisting black soldiers, amending the Constitution to abolish slavery, allowing some African Americans to vote—Lincoln came to occupy positions the abolitionists had first staked out. The destruction of slavery during the Civil War offers an example, as relevant today as in Lincoln's time, of how the combination of an engaged social movement and an enlightened political leader can produce far-reaching social change.

Lincoln did not elaborate his views on slavery until the 1850s, when he emerged as a major spokesman for the newly-created Republican Party, committed to halting the westward expansion of slavery. In speeches of eloquence and power, Lincoln condemned slavery as a fundamental violation of the founding principles of the United States, as enunciated in the Declaration of Independence—the affirmation of human equality and of the natural right to life, liberty, and the pursuit of happiness. To Lincoln, equality meant the equal right to the fruits of one's labor, in a society that offered opportunity for advancement to what he and others called the "free laborer."

There are many grounds for condemning the institution of

slavery—moral, religious, political, economic. Lincoln referred to all of them at one time or another, but ultimately saw slavery as a form of theft—stealing the labor of one person and appropriating it for another. Lincoln was frequently charged by Democrats with supporting "Negro equality." He firmly denied the charge, as we will see. But he explained the kind of equality in which he did believe, using a black woman as an illustration: "In some respects she certainly is not my equal; but in her natural right to eat the bread she earns with her own hand without asking the leave of anyone else, she is my equal, and the equal of all others."[2] The natural right to the fruits of one's labor was the grounding of equality, not bounded by either race or gender.

Lincoln could declare, "I have always hated slavery, I think as much as any Abolitionist."[3] He used language similar to that of abolitionism—he spoke of slavery as a "monstrous injustice," a cancer that threatened the lifeblood of the nation.[4] Why then, was he not an abolitionist? Before the Civil War, abolitionists were a small, despised group. Outside a few districts, no one with political ambitions could be an abolitionist. If you were from central Illinois, abolitionism was hardly a viable political position.

I am not saying, however, that Lincoln was a secret abolitionist restrained by political pragmatism. Abolitionists believed that the moral issue of slavery was the paramount issue confronting the nation, overriding everything else. This was not Lincoln's view. In a famous letter to his Kentucky friend Joshua Speed, in 1855, Lincoln recalled their visit in 1841 to St. Louis, where they encountered slavery: "That sight was a continual torment to me; and I see something like it every time I touch the Ohio [River, the boundary between free and slave states].... You ought ... to appreciate how much the great body of the northern people do crucify their feelings, in order to maintain their loyalty to the constitution and the Union." Just before this sentence, Lincoln commented on fugitive slaves: "I confess I hate to see the poor creatures hunted down, and caught, and carried back to their stripes, and unrewarded toils; but I bite my lip and keep quiet."[5]

Why did he keep silent? Because the right to recover fugitives is in the Constitution.

William Lloyd Garrison burned the Constitution because of its clauses protecting slavery. Lincoln revered the Constitution.

He believed the United States had a mission to exemplify the institutions of democracy and self-government for the entire world. This, of course, was the theme of the Gettysburg Address. He was not, to be sure, a believer in "manifest destiny"—the idea that Americans had a God-given right to acquire new territory in the name of liberty, regardless of the desires of the actual inhabitants. Lincoln saw American democracy as an example to the world, not something to be imposed on others by unilateral force.

The combination of hatred of slavery and reverence for the Constitution created a serious dilemma for Lincoln, and for many others. In his great Peoria speech of 1854, Lincoln explained that slavery "deprives our republican example of its just influence in the world—enables the enemies of free institutions, with plausibility, to taunt us as hypocrites—causes the real friends of freedom to doubt our sincerity." Slavery, in other words, was an obstacle to the fulfillment of the historic mission of the United States. Yet, the nation's unity must be maintained, even if it meant compromising with slavery. Certainly, the compromises of the Constitution, including very distasteful ones like the fugitive slave clause, could not be violated lest the entire edifice fall to pieces.[6]

Another key difference between Lincoln and abolitionists lay in their views regarding race. Abolitionists insisted that once freed, slaves should be recognized as equal members of the American republic. They viewed the struggles against slavery and racism as intimately connected. Lincoln saw slavery and racism as distinct questions. Unlike his Democratic opponents in the North and pro-slavery advocates in the South, Lincoln claimed for blacks the natural rights to which all persons were entitled. "I think the negro," he wrote in 1858, "is included in the word 'men' used in the Declaration of Independence," and that slavery was therefore wrong.[7] But inalienable natural rights—life, liberty, the pursuit of happiness—he insisted, did not necessarily carry with them civil, political, or social equality. Persistently charged with belief in "Negro equality" during his campaign for the Senate against Stephen A. Douglas, Lincoln responded that he was not "nor ever have been, in favor of making voters or jurors of Negroes, nor of qualifying them to hold office, nor to intermarry with white people."[8] Lincoln refused to condemn the notorious Black Laws of Illinois, which made it a crime for black persons to enter the state.

Throughout the 1850s and for the first half of the Civil War, Lincoln believed that "colonization"—that is, encouraging black people to emigrate to a new homeland in Africa, the Caribbean, or Central America—ought to accompany the end of slavery. We sometimes forget how widespread the belief in colonization was in the pre-Civil War era. Henry Clay and Thomas Jefferson, the statesmen most revered by Lincoln, outlined plans to accomplish it. Rather than a fringe movement, it was part of a widely-shared mainstream solution to the issues of slavery and race. [9]

Colonization allowed its proponents to think about the end of slavery without confronting the question of the place of blacks in a post-emancipation society. Why should freed slaves leave the country? Clay had a reason: he spoke of free blacks as a "debased and degraded set," and insisted that multiplying their numbers would pose a danger to American society.[10] Lincoln never said anything like this—he did not verbally abuse black people as so many Northern politicians, including some Republicans, did. Jefferson had a different reason. As he explained in his famous letter to Edward Coles about prospects for ending slavery, while the institution must come to an end, if the two races lived together as free people, "amalgamation" would follow.[11] Jefferson practiced amalgamation but feared its consequences. Lincoln never said anything about this either. Instead, Lincoln emphasized the strength of white racism. Because of it, he said several times, blacks could never achieve equality in the United States. They should remove themselves to a homeland where they could fully enjoy freedom and self-government.[12]

Many scholars have been puzzled by Lincoln's public advocacy of colonization, or have simply ignored it, insisting that Lincoln could not have been serious when he advanced the idea, which does not fit easily with the image of the Great Emancipator. It is important to remember that for Clay, Lincoln, and many others, colonization was part of a broader program for ending slavery in a political system that erected seemingly insuperable legal and constitutional barriers to abolition.

To oversimplify, slavery can be abolished in one of three ways. One is individual manumission, some of which occurred in the United States but not nearly enough to threaten the system's viability. Second is emancipation by legal means. This can proceed where owners lack the political power to prevent it, as happened in the northern states after the American Revolution, and in the British Empire. Where the owners are more powerful, legal abolition requires their consent. Lincoln, like Clay, long believed that this could be obtained only through a program of gradual emancipation, coupled with monetary compensation to the owners for their loss of property in slaves, and a plan to encourage (or, in the case of Clay and Jefferson, require) blacks to leave the country, as it seemed impossible that slaveholders would ever consent to the creation of a vast new population of free African Americans.

The third mode of emancipation is military emancipation. War destabilizes slavery; it strips away its constitutional protections. Contending sides make slavery a military target to weaken their opponents. They enlist slave soldiers. This happened many times in wars in the Western Hemisphere, including during the American Revolution. It would happen during the Civil War. But in the 1850s, no one knew war was on the horizon; no one could conceive of a way of ending slavery without the cooperation of slaveholders. The Constitution barred interference with slavery in the states where it already existed. For Lincoln, as for most Republicans, anti-slavery action meant not attacking slavery where it was, but working to prevent its westward expansion. (I suppose there is a fourth mode of emancipation—slave revolution, as in Haiti. But this was highly unusual and certainly no one in the United States thought it was a likely occurrence except perhaps John Brown.)

Lincoln, however, did talk about a future without slavery. The aim of the Republican Party, he insisted, was to put the institution on the road to "ultimate extinction," a phrase he borrowed from Henry Clay. To the white South, Lincoln seemed as dangerous as an abolitionist, because he was committed to the eventual end of slavery. This was why it was the election not of Garrison or Phillips but of Lincoln—a mainstream Republican politician—that led inexorably to secession and civil war. The Southern secession conventions made it clear that they feared Lincoln's administration would be a threat to the future of slavery.

During the Civil War, of course, Lincoln had to do more than talk about slavery. He had to act. How did he become, if indeed he did become, the Great Emancipator?

The Civil War, of course, did not begin as a crusade to abolish slavery. Almost from the beginning, however, abolitionists and Radical Republicans pressed for action against slavery as a war measure. Faced with this pressure, Lincoln began to put forward his own ideas. I do not wish to rehearse in detail the complicated chronology of events in 1861 and 1862. In summary, Lincoln first proposed gradual, voluntary emancipation coupled with colonization—a plan that would make slave-owners partners in abolition. Lincoln has been criticized for delay in moving toward emancipation. I do not believe this is correct. In August 1861, he willingly signed the First Confiscation Act, which emancipated slaves employed for military labor by the Confederacy. In November 1861, only a few months into the war, when no significant battle had yet been fought, he met with political leaders from Delaware to present his plan. Delaware was one of the four border slave states (along with Maryland, Kentucky, and Missouri) that remained in the Union. In 1860, it had only eighteen hundred slaves. Delaware, Lincoln said, could have the glory of leading the way to the end of slavery. It would be gradual, compensated, and the government would encourage the freed slaves to emigrate. Delaware was not interested. Slave-owners do not wish to relinquish their slaves, even for compensation. (Ironically, Delaware, with Kentucky, were the last states to see slavery end—only the ratification of the Thirteenth Amendment abolished the institution there.) Undeterred, throughout the spring and summer of 1862, Lincoln promoted his plan with the border states, and any Confederates willing to listen, to no avail.[13]

    Lincoln's plan also fell apart at the other end—among blacks. In August 1862, he held a famous meeting with black leaders from Washington, D. C. Lincoln was only the second president to meet with blacks in a capacity other than slaves or servants. The first time came half a century earlier, when James Madison met with the black sea captain Paul Cuffe, who wanted to promote emigration to Africa. Lincoln's purpose was the same. At the meeting he issued a powerful indictment of slavery—blacks, he said, were suffering "the greatest wrong ever inflicted on any people." But he refused to issue a similar condemnation of racism; nor did he associate himself with it: "Whether it is right or wrong I need not discuss." Racism was intractable. "Even when you cease to be slaves, you are yet far removed from being placed on an equality with the white race.... It is better for us both, therefore, to be separated."[14] But the large majority of black Americans refused to contemplate emigration from the land of their birth. They insisted on their right to remain here and fight for equality.

In mid-1862 Congress moved ahead of Lincoln on emancipation, although he signed all their measures: the abolition of slavery in the territories; abolition in the District of Columbia (with around three hundred dollars compensation for each slaveowner); the Second Confiscation Act of July 1862, which freed all slaves of pro-Confederate owners in areas thenceforth occupied by the Union army and slaves of such owners who escaped to Union lines. Meanwhile, Lincoln was moving toward his own plan of emancipation. A powerful combination of events propelled him, among them:

The failure of efforts to fight the Civil War as a conventional war without targeting the bedrock of Southern society. Military stalemate generated support in the North, first among abolitionists and then more broadly, for making slavery a military target. A war of army against army must become a war of society against society.

Many Northerners feared that Britain might recognize the Confederacy or even intervene on its behalf. Adding emancipation to preserving the Union as a war aim would prevent this.

Slavery itself was beginning to disintegrate. From the beginning, the slaves saw the Civil War as heralding the long-awaited dawn of freedom. Hundreds, then thousands, ran away to Union lines. Slaves realized that the war had changed the balance of power in the South. Their actions forced the administration to begin to devise policies with regard to slavery.

Enthusiasm for enlistment was waning rapidly in the North. By 1863, a draft would be authorized. At the beginning of the war, the army had refused to accept black volunteers. But the reservoir of black manpower could no longer be ignored.

All these pressures moved Lincoln in the direction of general emancipation. He first proposed this to his Cabinet on July

22, 1862. Two months later, in September 1862, after General George McClellan's army forced Confederates under Robert E. Lee to retreat from Maryland at the battle of Antietam, Lincoln issued the Preliminary Emancipation Proclamation—essentially a warning to the South to lay down its arms or face emancipation in one hundred days. In the interim, Lincoln continued to pursue his colonization idea (which was specifically mentioned in the Preliminary Proclamation).

The Emancipation Proclamation, issued on January 1, 1863, is perhaps the most misunderstood important document in American history. Certainly, it is untrue that Lincoln freed 4 million slaves with a stroke of his pen. The Proclamation had no bearing on the slaves in the four border states. Since they remained in the Union, the constitutional protections of slavery remained in place for them. The Proclamation exempted certain areas of the Confederacy that had fallen under Union military control, including parts of Virginia and Louisiana and the entire state of Tennessee (this was at the request of military governor Andrew Johnson—it was a significant exaggeration to say that all of Tennessee was in Union hands). All told, perhaps 800,000 of the nearly 4 million slaves were not covered by the Proclamation. But 3.1 million were. This was the largest emancipation in world history. Never before had so many slaves been declared free on a single day. The Proclamation did not end slavery when it was issued, but it sounded the death knell of slavery in the United States—assuming the Union won the war (were the Confederacy to emerge victorious, slavery would undoubtedly last a long time). Everybody recognized that if slavery perished in South Carolina, Alabama, and Mississippi, it could hardly survive in Tennessee, Kentucky, and a few parishes of Louisiana.

A military measure whose constitutional legitimacy rested on the "war power" of the president, the Emancipation Proclamation often proves disappointing to those who read it. Unlike the Declaration of Independence, it contains no soaring language, no immortal preamble enunciating the rights of man. Couched in dull, legalistic language, much of it consists of a long quotation from the Preliminary Proclamation of September. Only at the last moment, at the urging of abolitionist Secretary of the Treasury Salmon P. Chase, did Lincoln add a conclusion declaring the proclamation not only an exercise of "military necessity," but "an act of justice."[15]

Nonetheless, the Proclamation was the turning point of the Civil War and in Lincoln's understanding of his own role in history. Lincoln was not the Great Emancipator, if by that we mean someone who was waiting all his life to abolish slavery. He was not the Great Emancipator if this means that he freed four million slaves in an instant. One might better say that Lincoln became the Great Emancipator—that he assumed the role thrust on him by history, and henceforth tried to live up to it. Lincoln knew he would be remembered for this act. The Preliminary Proclamation had included a long excerpt from the Second Confiscation Act, leaving the impression that Lincoln was acting on congressional authority. The Emancipation Proclamation made no mention of any congressional legislation. Lincoln claimed full authority as commander-in-chief to decree emancipation, and accepted full responsibility.

Lincoln had said, in his December 1862 message to Congress, "We must disenthrall ourselves, and then we shall save our country." He included himself in that "we." The Emancipation Proclamation was markedly different from Lincoln's previous statements and policies regarding slavery. It abandoned the idea of seeking the cooperation of slaveholders in emancipation, and of distinguishing between loyal and disloyal owners. It was immediate, not gradual, contained no mention of compensation for slave-owners, and made no reference to colonization. For the first time, it authorized the enrollment of black soldiers into the Union army. The Proclamation set in motion the process by which two hundred thousand black men served in the Union army and navy during the last two years of the war, playing a critical role in achieving Union victory.

Lincoln would, on occasion, refer to elements of his previous thinking, such as gradualism and compensation, in the next two years. But from January 1, 1863 onward, he never again mentioned colonization in public. And while his administration continued to offer assistance to blacks who voluntarily decided to emigrate, colonization was no longer part of a larger program of abolition. Since emancipation no longer required the consent of slaveholders, colonization had become irrelevant. Moreover, putting black men into the army implied a very different vision of their future place in American society. You do not ask men to fight and die for the Union and then send them and their families out of the country.

One of the pleasures of working on Lincoln is simply reading, slowly and carefully, his writings. He was an extremely careful writer, with a remarkable command of the English language. Even the familiar Emancipation Proclamation itself produces surprises when read with care. The Preliminary Proclamation had aroused criticism for seeming to encourage violence by the slaves. In the final version, Lincoln enjoined the former slaves to refrain from violence, but he added, "except in necessary self-defense." Lincoln was not cowed by widespread charges that emancipation would be followed by a racial bloodbath. Lincoln did not have to say that blacks had a right to defend their freedom by violence if need be, but he did so. And, repudiating his earlier commitment to colonization without quite saying so, he urged freed slaves to go to work for "reasonable wages"—in the United States. Not just wages, but reasonable wages. Lincoln wanted to make clear that the former slaves had a right to compete in the marketplace as free laborers, to judge for themselves the wages offered them. In other words, in the Proclamation, Lincoln addressed African Americans directly, not as the property of the nation's enemies, but as men and women with volition, whose loyalty the Union must earn.[16]

Overall, the Proclamation fundamentally changed the character of the Civil War. It made the destruction of slavery a purpose of the Union army. It liquidated without compensation the largest concentration of property in the United States. It crystallized a new identification between the ideal of liberty and a nation-state whose powers increased enormously as the war progressed.

Lincoln came to emancipation more slowly than the abolitionists desired. But having made the decision, he did not look back. In 1864, with casualties mounting, there was talk of a compromise peace. Some urged Lincoln to rescind the Proclamation, in which case, they believed, the South could be persuaded to return to the Union. At the least, some Republican leaders insisted, such a step could defuse opposition to his reelection, which was very much in jeopardy that summer. Lincoln would not consider this. Were he to do so, he told one visitor,

"I should be damned in time and eternity."[17] (Had McClellan defeated Lincoln in 1864, it is quite possible to imagine the Union being restored with slavery still existing in some places.)

Lincoln knew full well that the Proclamation depended for its effectiveness on Union victory, that it did not apply to all slaves, and that its constitutionality was certain to be challenged in the future. In the last two years of the war he worked to secure complete abolition, pressing the border states to take action against slavery on their own (which Maryland and Missouri did), requiring that Southerners who wished to have their other property restored pledge to support emancipation, and working to secure congressional passage of the Thirteenth Amendment. None of these measures, when adopted, included gradualism, compensation, or colonization.

Moreover, by decoupling emancipation from colonization, Lincoln in effect launched the historical process known as Reconstruction—the remaking of southern society, politics, and race relations. Lincoln did not live to see Reconstruction implemented and eventually abandoned. But in the last two years of the war, he came to recognize that if emancipation settled one question, the fate of slavery, it opened another: What was to be the role of emancipated slaves in post-war American life?

In 1863 and 1864, Lincoln for the first time began to think seriously on this question. Two of Lincoln's final pronouncements show how his thinking was evolving. One was his "last speech," delivered at the White House in April 1865 a few days before his assassination. Of course, Lincoln did not know this was his last speech—it should not be viewed as a final summation of policy. In it he addressed Reconstruction, already underway in Louisiana. A new constitution had been ratified, which abolished slavery yet limited voting rights to whites. The state's free black community complained bitterly about their exclusion from the ballot, with support from Radical Republicans in the North. Most northern states at this point, however, did not allow blacks to vote and most Republicans felt that it would be politically suicidal to endorse black suffrage. In this speech, Lincoln announced that he would "prefer" that limited black suffrage be implemented. He singled out not only the "very intelligent"—the free blacks—but also "those who serve our cause as soldiers" as most worthy. Moreover, he noted that blacks desired the right to vote—an indication that their opinions were now part of the political equation. Hardly an unambiguous embrace of equality, this was the first time that an American president had publically endorsed any kind of political rights for blacks. Lincoln was telling the country that the service of black soldiers, inaugurated by the Emancipation Proclamation, entitled them a political voice in the reunited nation.[18]

Then there is one of the greatest speeches in American history, Lincoln's second inaugural address, of March 4, 1865. Today, it is remembered for its closing words: "with malice toward none, with charity for all … let us strive to bind up the nation's wounds." But before that noble ending, Lincoln tried to instruct his fellow countrymen on the historical significance of the war and the unfinished task that still remained.

It must have been very tempting, with Union victory imminent, for Lincoln to view the outcome as the will of God and to blame the war on the sins of the Confederacy. Yet Lincoln said he would not even discuss events on the battlefield; rather he dwelled on the deep meaning of the war. Everybody knew, he noted, that slavery was "somehow" the cause of the Civil War. Not the black presence, as he had said in his meeting with the blacks from Washington, D. C. in 1862, but slavery as an institution. Yet Lincoln called it "American slavery," not southern slavery, underscoring the entire nation's complicity. No man, he continued, truly knows God's will. Men wanted the war to end, but God might wish it to continue as a punishment to the nation for the sin of slavery, "until all the wealth piled by the bond-man's 250 years of unrequited toil shall be sunk, and until every drop of blood drawn with the lash, shall be paid by another drawn by the sword."[19] Here was a final reaffirmation of his definition of slavery as a theft of labor, and also one of the very few times that Lincoln spoke publically of the physical brutality inherent in slavery (Lincoln generally discussed slavery as an abstraction, a matter of principle, rather than dwelling on its day-to-day brutality). Lincoln was reminding his audience that the "terrible" violence of the Civil War had been preceded by 250 years of the terrible violence of slavery. Violence, then, did not begin with the firing on Fort Sumter in April 1861.

In essence, Lincoln was asking the entire nation to confront unblinkingly the legacy of the long history of bondage. What are the requirements of justice in the face of this reality? What is the nation's obligation for those 250 years of unpaid labor? What is necessary to enable the former slaves, their children, and their descendants to enjoy the "pursuit of happiness" he had always insisted was their natural right, but which had so long been denied to them? Within a few weeks, Lincoln was dead. He did not provide an answer. And 150 years after the Emancipation Proclamation, these questions continue to bedevil American society.

Notes

[1] Eric Foner, The Fiery Trial: Abraham Lincoln and American Slavery (New York, 2010).
[2] Roy P. Basler, ed., The Collected Works of Abraham Lincoln (8 vols: New Brunswick, 1953-55), 2: 405.
[3] Ibid., 2: 492.
[4] Ibid., 2: 252; 3: 313.
[5] Ibid., 2: 320.
[6] Ibid., 2: 255-56.
[7] Ibid., 3: 327.
[8] Ibid., 3: 145.
[9] Eric Foner, "Lincoln and Colonization," in Foner, ed., Our Lincoln: New Perspectives on Lincoln and His World (New York, 2008), 135-66.
[10] James F. Hopkins, ed., Papers of Henry Clay (10 vols.: Lexington, 1959-91), 10: 844-46.
[11] John C. Miller, Wolf By the Ears: Thomas Jefferson and Slavery (New York, 1977), 207.
[12] Basler, Collected Works, 2: 256.
[13] Foner, Fiery Trial, 181-84, 212-13.
[14] Basler, Collected Works, 5: 371-75.
[15] Basler, Collected Works, 6: 30.
[16] Ibid., 6: 30; Foner, Fiery Trial, 219.
[17] Basler, Collected Works, 7: 507.
[18] Ibid., 8: 403.
[19] Ibid., 8: 332-33.

The Shape of Freedom

Edward L. Ayers

I would like to build a bridge between Eric's discussion of Lincoln and our broader examination of the home front. I want to show how deeply entangled the home front was with war-making and with the process that ultimately brought the end of slavery, to show the contours of the home front and the patterns that marked the end of slavery. As a way toward seeing those patterns, I want to introduce the mapping project that we have created at the University of Richmond: *Visualizing Emancipation*. (dsl.richmond.edu/emancipation)

The small dots you see on the map are units of the United States army at different points during the war. The large dots are everywhere we have documented an interaction of African-American people with that army. Most of the information in *Visualizing Emancipation* is from the *Official Records of the War of the Rebellion* and their summary in the *Dyer Compendium*; and you will notice that every major theater, campaign, and battle is represented here, as well as these interactions. The thirty-five hundred large dots document every time the United States army mentions that it interacts with a "colored, free, slave, [or] Negro" person. We have then augmented that information for Virginia to include runaway slave ads, diaries, and letters.

16 / *The American Civil War at Home*

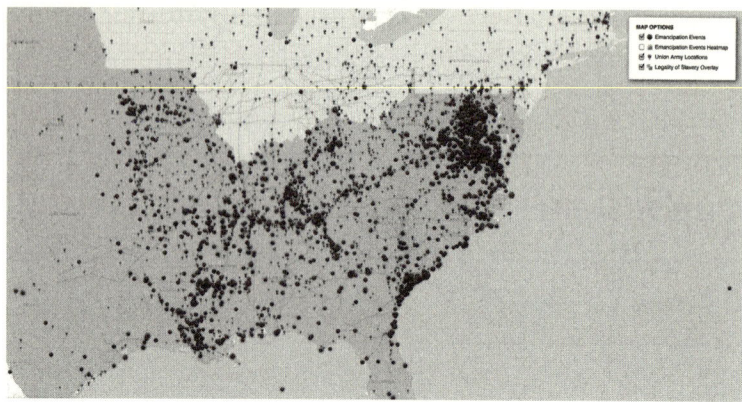

Screen capture, *Visualizing Emancipation*, University of Richmond. dsl.richmond.edu/emancipation

This is what the end of slavery looks like. It is not waiting for 1865 and it is not waiting for the Thirteenth Amendment. The end of slavery starts at the very beginning of the war. Every one of the large dots is a story that you can click on to see the individual account behind it. These stories can help to answer questions that historians continue to argue about: What role did Abraham Lincoln play in ending slavery? What role did the United States army play? What role did the enslaved people themselves play? These are still frontiers of new knowledge that we're trying to explore, but several basic patterns are clear.

First of all, as you can see, the geographic immensity of the social drama that was emancipation was overwhelming. The Confederacy covered an area the size of continental Europe, and the end of slavery does not arrive at one time or place. When we talk about the home front, two images of a "front" might come in mind: a military front or a meteorological front. Neither one fits here, however: no line marked a clear division between where the war was and where it was not, where danger and devastation reigned and where they were absent. *Visualizing Emancipation* shows, in other words, the vastness of the end of slavery, and how many people and hands were involved in bringing that end.

The second pattern to notice is the long chronological span of slavery's end. Three weeks after Virginia secedes, African Americans begin making themselves free. Within weeks, after 250 years of slavery, three enslaved men row across the harbor to

Fortress Monroe and seek out whatever allies they can find. You can see that the same process is happening wherever the United States army goes. You can see it all along the coast in the Carolinas, and also along the Mississippi and the Tennessee, in Mobile Bay, in Louisiana, and out west in Missouri. African Americans are fleeing to anywhere that there might be an ally.

The home front, then, is everywhere the war is. It is not some place where you are either in the war or you are not. You can be in the war any day that you wake up, when the railroad brings in Union troops or when it brings in the Confederates, no matter where you might be. The home front is where there is an army eating your food or taking away your livestock. It is anywhere that you might find your son conscripted or your daughter harassed.

The third point to notice is the wildly uneven patterns of interaction across different parts of the South. Here in Virginia, for example, Williamsburg was a battle site early in the war and then occupied throughout. Appomattox, however, was barely touched by the war and slavery was barely disrupted until the very end of the conflict. The home front is remarkably complicated and a distance of just one hundred miles could shape the entire experience of what the Civil War might mean for you, your family, your farm, or your town—even here in Virginia, which is occupied, fought over, and disrupted from start to finish.

Included in the *Visualizing Emancipation* map is a drop-down menu with different Emancipation Event Types. These Event Types reflect the different situations an enslaved person taking the risk to become free might find himself in, because he cannot know what those Union soldiers are going to be like when he gets to Union encampments. Imagine an eighteen year-old woman with a baby. She finally hears that the Yankees are two miles away and she makes a break for it. Some of the many things that could happen are listed in the Emancipation Event Types. She could be abused, or raped. She could find herself in a camp outside the army, camps not made to take in thousands of refugees. She might find the Confederates tracking her down and dragging her back home or making her work for them. This means that these large dots are not necessarily places where the Union army came in and bestowed freedom. It means that there was a place that African Americans risked everything to see if they might be able to seize freedom out

18 / *The American Civil War at Home*

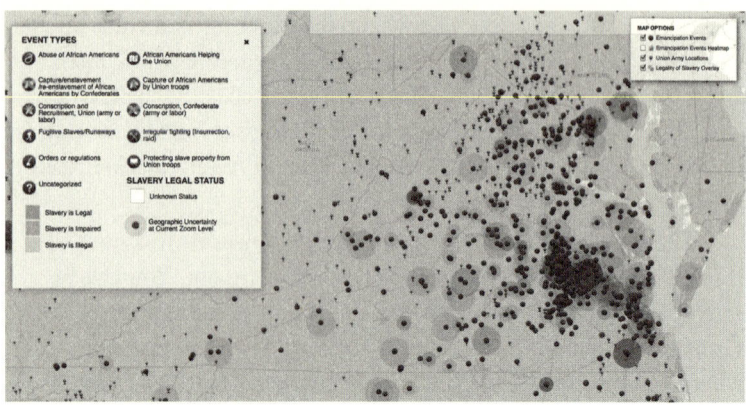

Screen capture, *Visualizing Emancipation*, University of Richmond. dsl.richmond.edu/emancipation

of this fleeting moment.

The map shows a number of different circumstances, including when the army leaves. We see the home front, the war, washing over Virginia. Williamsburg is occupied once, while Winchester is occupied many times. Richmond is completely disrupted by the war from start to finish as the fronts shift all around it. Another element still is the enormous role of disease among the enslaved people who are trying to make themselves free. Even further, it mattered a lot if you were a man or a woman, young or old, able-bodied or ill. It mattered a lot if you had children to be responsible for, if you happened to be on a plantation where there was a large group of your family or loved ones, or if you were relatively new and a stranger.

Your experience might differ depending on whether the nearby units of the Union army were made up of men from New England or the Midwest, the political beliefs of the Union commander in charge, or whether the Confederate army felt it could afford the time and energy to round up enslaved people. One of the things that the United States army discovered early on in fighting around Williamsburg is that African Americans were helping them. The large dots, and the records on which they are based, show us that from the very beginning, as soon as the United States army came into contact with African Americans, soldiers consider them to be friends. They feel that African Americans were the only ones they could trust to tell them where to ford a river or which fork they should take in a road.

These words start getting back up to Washington. Two things are going to have to happen, according to the army: African Americans need to be freed because they are intelligent and determined, and they also need to be freed because they are being forced to aid the Confederates. The earthworks on which the sons of the Union are dying as they try to fight up the peninsula to Richmond are being dug by the forced labor of enslaved men. The Union soldiers discover that if they are going to defeat the Confederacy, they are going to have to control this part of the home front: this highly mobile, easily mobilized, and heavily exploited group of labor. United States soldiers are dying in the malarial heat of Virginia summers and the Confederates are in the shade, forcing their slave men to work. This reality leads Lincoln to change his mind because the enslaved people themselves are forcing him and enticing him. The reports from the United States army are saying that if the Union hopes to win the war, it is going to need to tap into the latent power, the possibility, the idealism, the bravery of the enslaved people around them.

The home front was remembered by white Virginians as a dismal and horrible time in which the Yankees came in and desecrated the South. It was remembered by African Americans as a time when they were able to go to Hampton and create their own city, their own village. They see that they can begin creating their own schools and their own churches to get a new start on life. They will not wait for the Emancipation Proclamation, or the Thirteenth Amendment. They will not even wait for Union victory. They will seize all that they can from the home front while they can.

There is, however, one important point to remember. Despite all the large dots, of the 4 million people held in slavery at the beginning of the war, 3.5 million have not come in contact with the United States army by the end of the war. Despite all that I have covered, giving some sense of the immensity of slavery, the fact remains that if you do not have the Thirteenth Amendment, if you do not have Reconstruction, slavery has only begun to end. What shape freedom might have is not clear at all. Seeing this process only from the top down is inadequate, but we cannot only imagine it from the bottom up either. We have to realize that laws and policies matter profoundly. We see that slavery cannot be divorced from military history, political history, or legal history. Neither can it be divorced from the role of gender, economic life, and geography itself. Fortunately, that kind of integrated understanding, that kind of humane and capacious comprehension of all that the home front was, all that the war was, all that emancipation was, is exactly what we are here to talk about today.

ENSLAVED WOMEN AND THE BATTLE FOR FREEDOM AND DEMOCRACY IN THE CIVIL WAR

THAVOLIA GLYMPH

> *Since the date of my last report the forces under my command have broken up the plantations engaged in raising cotton under Federal leases from Milliken's Bend to Lake Providence, capturing some 2,000 negroes, who have been restored to their masters, with the exception of those captured in arms, and a few the property of disloyal citizens of Louisiana. . . . I am now engaged in burning all the cotton I can reach from Lake Providence to the lower end of Concordia Parish.... I have also instructed the cavalry to destroy all subsistence and forage on abandoned plantations.*
>
> Confederate General J.G.Walker
> Report from Delhi, LA, July 10, 1863

From the moment the American Civil War began, enslaved men, women, and children started moving to shape the contours of the war, and its meaning. Until the war's end, their objective was unchanged: emancipation and the advancement of freedom and democracy in the United States. In 1861, however, they stood virtually alone in believing that the Civil War could possibly result in their freedom. For most Americans the question of emancipation was not a part of the equation that led to war. The Confederate States of America, for its part, was founded on the ambition of building a pro-slavery nation state and the Union went to war simply to restore the Union as it had been. Refusing the legitimacy of both views, enslaved people ran toward Union armies that had not come to free them. They offered their services as military laborers, scouts, spies, cooks, and nurses to a nation that regarded their politics as a distraction and, ultimately, a political, social, and financial burden. At first, Union commanders determinately sent them away and allowed slaveholders to enter their camps to retrieve slaves they asserted belonged to them. Before long, however, the need for additional bodies to bear shovels and build fortifications and canals, to serve as military cooks and nurses, laundresses, and firemen on naval boats fueled the emergence of a different consensus: the Union war must inescapably touch the enslaved. Union commanders and soldiers facing Confederate fortifications built with the coerced labor of enslaved men increasingly joined the voices calling for the employment of the enslaved in support of the Union cause.

Still, the emerging consensus on the value of African-American labor to the Union cause initially did not embrace emancipation as an ancillary goal. Inclusion of the enslaved, most white Northerners continued to believe, need not encompass emancipation or any plan to reconstruct the nation on the basis of equality. Rather, they believed, as Lincoln did, that their own racism would make it impossible for black people to lead fully free lives in the United States, a position on view in Lincoln's advocacy of colonization. By the time he issued the final Emancipation Proclamation, of course, the president had shed this idea for all practical purposes. The Proclamation did not link black freedom to colonization and called, moreover, for the enlistment of black men as soldiers in the US army, paving the path for their claims to freedom and citizenship.

The Emancipation Proclamation thus represented an acknowledgment of just how important the slaves' war had become to the Union cause. Yet, while black men's contributions as soldiers and military laborers to the Union cause came into sharper focus, what part enslaved women would play remained dimly perceived, the gradual inclusion of their right to freedom as a condition of their relationship to black soldier husbands notwithstanding. But the slaves' war—from flight to Union military lines to struggle on the plantations to re-shape the terrain of slavery and bend it towards freedom—was also a slave woman's war.

The history of women in the Civil War has largely been told

as a story of white women's sacrifice—of sons and husbands and fathers—and of "home." It has elucidated the stories of white women who went to the front as nurses and as missionaries and agents for soldiers' and freedmen's aid societies, and those who became refugees. It has chronicled the property losses they suffered through the actions of Union and Confederate armies on the move, the home front scarcities and making-do, and the difficulties faced by women forced to work for the first time in their lives. Of course, these stories have never suffered a lack of chroniclers. Histories of white women began rolling off the press before the war ended and remained popular subjects in the decades that followed. In more recent decades, however, revisionist scholarship has challenged the traditional narrative, complicating and transforming it in critically important ways. The Confederate story and its class and race dimensions, for example, looks different when the lives of poor white women and enslaved women form part of the narrative, as does the story of the Union. My interest is in thinking, in particular, about how we tell the story of Southern black women in the Civil War.

Long dominated by the narratives of a few well-known black women—Sojourner Truth, Susie King Taylor, Harriet Tubman, Mary Peake, Harriet Jacobs, and Charlotte Forten—the scholarship on black women in the Civil War has advanced considerably in recent years to encompass the lives of "ordinary" black women. From the margins of Civil War history, the tens of thousands of enslaved women who fled the South's plantations and farms and forced their way onto the national agenda increasingly occupy a place near, if not at, the center. The history of the war that is being re-written follows these women from the sites of their enslavement to Union camps where some found work as cooks, nurses, laundresses, and woodchoppers, some as laborers on abandoned plantations confiscated by the federal government. Yet for these refugees from slavery, freedom proved contingent and finding a place of safe refuge elusive. An untold number died on the Civil War's battlefields, along with their children, from military fire, poor nutrition, and disease, and found themselves re-enslaved by Confederate forces that attacked the refugee camps and Federal plantations.

An African-American refugee camp in Helena. T.W. Bankes, photographer, Nebraska State Historical Society, RG3323 PH6-8.

Enslaved women and children who made it to Union lines and refugee camps with the expectation of freedom and safe refuge regularly encountered inept or disinterested Union commanders and soldiers, and an array of "contraband" policies that often varied from one command to the next. To the end of the war, some Federal commanders continued to turn them out of Union lines, protest their claims to protection, deny them access to military rations (or reduce them to starvation levels) and other supplies, send them back to slavery, and open their camps to slaveholders even in the face of congressional law and Federal policies forbidding such acts. Commanders more sympathetic to the plight the refugees faced who opened their liens to black women and children were often unable to provide adequate medical care or to adequately protect them from either Confederate raids or Treasury Department officials who looked to black women as a source of labor to gather abandoned cotton and cultivate new cash crops. Although the Freedmen's Department (a precursor to the Freedmen's Bureau) in the Mississippi Valley worked to bring some order to refugee life, its efforts were plagued by too few agents, inadequate supplies, and rampant corruption. Ultimately, the immensity of the crisis was no match for the resources at their disposal.

There was little to be done in instances when Union forces arrived on the scene too late to help. Such was the case at

Goodrich's Landing, Louisiana in the summer of 1863 where Confederate cavalry and artillery forces attacked refugee camps and captured twelve hundred people. Union colonel Samuel J. Nasmith's report detailed the atrocities that had taken place, the "charred remains" that testified to a fiendishness, he wrote, that had "no parallel either in civilized or savage warfare." Or when black men who worked as military laborers died in service and the government refused to pay their back wages to their widows or children. Or when the government taxed the meager wages of black women.

Violence against black women and children in its many forms—hunger, homelessness, new disease environments, family separations, and a growing population of orphaned children without the safety net of settled slave communities—fueled the Civil War's largest humanitarian crisis, alleviated only in small measure by the work of Northern and Southern freedmen's aid societies and sanitary commissions. The immensity of the task outstripped the resources they could bring to bear. Telling the story of this crisis is as important as telling the story of the discrimination and racism black soldiers faced and the battles they won; as important, too, as the story of white women rioters, refugees, slaveholders, soldiers, abolitionists, and missionaries.

Placing the story of black women in the narrative of the Civil War does not require that we find "new" archives or manuscripts. The "old" ones are more than sufficient to the task. It will require that we ask different questions of the sources and re-think the categories of analysis and methodologies that ground our questions. It will require that we continue to wrestle with the very meaning of the term "battlefield." We now have a body of rich scholarship that explores the muddling of the distinction between the home front and the battlefront and marks the home front as a site of war. Refugee camps, no less than planters' homes, are also best understood as battlefields and spaces of displacement and re-enslavement that were, simultaneously, places of hoped-for refuge.

We might profitably think about black women and children refugees in the Civil War, to borrow from the language of modern refugee studies, as occupying the status of "unrecognized refugees." This meaning was on view in the Western Sanitary Commission's contention that there were "two classes of sufferers" in the war-torn

South, only one of which it considered legitimate "Union refugees." They were white men, women, and children. "It would seem that no other plea can be needed," the commissioners wrote, "than the simple statement that they have been deprived of all their property, and have been driven from their homes, simply because they *would not be rebels*. We have all had to make sacrifices in this war for the Union, but what possible sacrifices can we have made, whose *homes* remain to us, which deserve to be mentioned in comparison with those which have fallen to the lot of these *impoverished* and *homeless Union refugees*."

Black women and children refugees were also impoverished and homeless. They too fled "because they *would not be rebels*." Yet their claims to freedom and refuge were more often debated than recognized. This remained true even after the Congressional Confiscation Acts that declared slaves of rebel Southerners free, the President's Emancipation Proclamation, and General Order No. 100 (Lieber Code), which proclaimed that a fugitive slave was "immediately entitled to the rights and privileges of a freeman" and came under "the shield of the law of nations." Instead, like that of many refugees today, the status of black women and children refugees approached what the Office of the United Nations High Commissioner for Refugees (UNHCR) defines as "protracted refugee status." Of course, neither the language of modern-day refugee scholarship nor the UNHCR policies and protocols of the twentieth and twenty-first centuries that today inform the status and rights of refugees were in place during the Civil War. Yet, attending to questions of asylum, displacement, citizenship and belonging, the meaning of wartime violence against women and children noncombatants, and the rights of noncombatants and even black women combatants within the context of the Civil War is critical to a fuller understanding of the Civil War, emancipation, and the making of freedom. By the end of the war, black women and children constituted the vast majority of the population in Civil War refugee camps. At Davis Bend, for example, they represented ninety percent of 2,325 refugees spread across eight camps in 1864. Their story and that of the tens of thousands like them is not only integral to the history of the war, emancipation, and the making of freedom, but to the war's long-term impact on the life chances of those who survived.

More Than Freedom: Black Northerners and the Meaning of Emancipation

Stephen Kantrowitz

We usually think of emancipation as a Civil War story, in which nearly four million African-American slaves achieved their freedom in a short span of years. But the legal dismantling of slavery had been taking place for generations prior to the Emancipation Proclamation, as states from Vermont to New Jersey set slavery on a gradual path to extinction. The result was a free black population of roughly a quarter of a million scattered across the villages, towns, and especially the cities of the North, nowhere making up more than a few percent of the population.

In my remarks today I am going to make a pair of linked arguments about this group of people. First, I am going to argue that their particular situation, as free but not equal people living under the shadow of racial slavery, taught them an important lesson about the limits of freedom and the need for a fuller sense of belonging in the American nation. Here, I will consider the challenges facing free black Northerners, their pursuit of white allies, and their militant and political campaign to secure equal rights and defend fugitive slaves. Second, I will show how these experiences and relationships, and especially their pursuit of equality, shaped black Northern activists' responses to the Civil War. In particular, I will try to show how it shaped the black military experience. Together, these arguments will explain how black Northerners turned bare freedom into equal citizenship. But they did more than this: for the first time in the nation's history, they made equality seem the natural offspring of freedom.

Free black Northerners were not slaves: they owned themselves and their labor; they could marry and raise children; they could hold property; offenses committed against them were crimes against them, not against an owner. Yet slavery shadowed their lives even after the Northern states brought the institution to an end between the 1770s and the 1840s. Nowhere were they fully equal under the law. Even in the four New England states where black men voted on the same basis as white men, they could not serve on juries or in the state militia. Elsewhere, they lacked the right to vote, or had that right gradually restricted or stripped from them outright during the 1820s and 1830s. Everywhere, they bore the stigma of racial slavery. Whites almost universally considered them less intelligent, less independent, and less worthy than themselves. Mobs chased them from the public squares, and sometimes expelled them entirely from cities and towns. The most popular entertainment of the mid-nineteenth century, blackface minstrelsy, was rooted in the mocking caricature of their lives, loves, and hopes. Perhaps most alarming of all, the most popular antislavery movement in the North (as in the South) was "colonization," a program of manumission and deportation in which owners freed individual slaves on the condition that they leave the country forever. Henry Clay, Whig Party leader, slaveholder, and perennial presidential candidate, was an ardent colonizationist; so was the Illinois politician who idolized him, Abraham Lincoln.

But this broad climate of scorn and hostility did not persuade most free black Northerners to leave the United States. Instead, they reached out to one another, and to their white neighbors. They first created congregations, mutual aid and burial societies, and Masonic lodges; by the late 1820s and 1830s, they started newspapers and assembled interstate conventions. Building on a hopeful reading of the universalist principles in Christian scripture and the Declaration of Independence, they began to articulate a vision of their future in the United States—one in which slavery would be no more, and they would be honored and esteemed members of society.

To achieve this they would need white allies to form a bridge between themselves and the hostile majority, and to provide a model for interracial interaction that others could emulate. This was part of what David Walker imagined in his landmark 1829 pamphlet, *Appeal to the Coloured Citizens*. A North Carolina migrant to Boston and a central figure in the Northern black activist world, Walker used his text to excoriate slavery and the evils it bred, including the colonization movement and the broad subjection of free blacks. But he also imagined a world of mutual regard and common destiny in fierce and yearning words: "Treat us like men, and there is no danger but we will all live in peace and happiness together. For we are not like you, hard hearted, unmerciful, and unforgiving. What a happy country this will be, if the whites will listen."

By the early 1830s, a handful of whites had begun to listen. Most notable among them was a newspaperman who, inspired by Walker's words and the aspirations of Boston's free black community, dedicated his life to the end of slavery and the coming of racial equality: William Lloyd Garrison. White women and men began to join together with their black neighbors to form societies that aimed not at deportation, but at the universal and immediate end of slavery. Some even took up the banner of equality, challenging the prejudices that their neighbors flaunted unashamedly, and which they themselves struggled to overcome. The people who called themselves abolitionists never made up more than a small fraction of white Northern society, but by challenging the assumption that the United States was a white man's republic, they left a profound mark upon it.

During the 1840s and 1850s, black and white activists together challenged both slavery and white supremacy. In petitions, protests, and political movements, they attacked slavery's extension into the West and the efforts of slaveholders to retrieve fugitives from the North. Black and white men and women defended those fugitives in print, in court, and in the streets, sometimes literally battling with slaveholders and agents of the state as they sought to prevent people from being returned to slavery.

In 1854, for example, in an effort to free the fugitive Anthony Burns, black and white men together beat down the door of the Boston Court House and killed a constable. They failed to rescue Burns, but they succeeded in another way: their resistance so unsettled federal authorities that they put thousands of soldiers and policemen in the streets to march the fugitive to the ship that

Courtesy of the Boston Athenaeum

returned him to slavery. The spectacle of armed force defending slaveholders' rights in the streets of Boston persuaded many non-abolitionist whites that they should join the abolitionists in their struggle against an overweening "Slave Power."

Black and white activists challenged the subordination and exclusion of black Northerners in every arena of life. In Massachusetts, black men were able to use the right to vote to enter into political alliances, which helped to secure the long-sought goal of desegregating the Boston public schools in 1855. There, too, black men sought admission to the state militia in a campaign led by pioneering African-American lawyer Robert Morris. The

Robert Morris, courtesy of the Social Law Library

leaders of the militia movement wanted to dress, drill, and march like the rest of the state militia, but they demanded that they be allowed to do so on terms of full equality. This required that the state ignore the federal militia law, which allowed only able-bodied white men to serve; and that it allow black men to serve as officers. The Massachusetts state government debated this petition many times, but it failed to become law. The company Robert Morris had assembled, the Massasoit Guard, dissolved in acrimony, never to don its uniforms in public or to march through the streets of Boston.

That disappointing denouement was not the end of the story, though, for the skills, commitments, and alliances developed over many decades surged into the new channels carved by the Civil War. By now we are familiar with the important role that black military service to the Union played in that conflict once the Emancipation Proclamation authorized their enlistment. Nearly two hundred thousand soldiers and sailors formed an important (indeed, by the end of the war, critical) addition to Union manpower. Of these, a sizeable minority were free men recruited in the Northern states. By the end of the war, an astonishing seventy-one percent of the eligible black men in the non-slave states served in arms, a proportion exceeded only by white Southern enrollment during the last desperate years of the Confederacy.

Black men's military service to the Union inspired great hope among black activists that the nation's need might result in their full acceptance as American citizens. "Once let the black man get upon his person the brass letters U.S.," predicted Frederick Douglass, "let him get an eagle on his button, and a musket on his shoulder ... [and] there is no power on the earth ... which can deny that he has earned the right of citizenship in the United States." Douglass recruited hundreds, including his two sons, to serve in the 54th Massachusetts and the scores of regiments soon to follow it into battle.

But Douglass's ringing words were, as yet, only a hope. It remained far from clear whether military service would bring equality as well as freedom. Indeed, from the very beginning, the call to service for black men was marred by repeated reminders of African Americans' subordinate position: in the years that elapsed before the Union assented to call on black men; in the refusal to commission them as officers; and in the ruling that they receive not the thirteen dollars a month due soldiers, but the lesser wage paid military laborers. All of these insults shaped how African Americans responded to the call for their service in 1863 and beyond. They provoked the same response from black activists that their peacetime subordination had brought: organization and protest, anchored by a demand for equality.

Morris and others seized the opening of black enlistment in early 1863 to demand that the first black regiment, the 54th Massachusetts, include black commissioned officers. Despite the entreaties of Massachusetts' abolitionist governor, Morris's longtime ally, the War Department would not bend. So at recruitment meetings in Boston, Morris argued that black men should refuse to serve until they could do so on terms of perfect equality. Morris's colleague William Wells Brown put it succinctly: "Equality first, guns afterward." Black and white recruiters in Boston, including Col. Robert Gould Shaw, the white commander of the 54th Massachusetts, complained bitterly about the success of their campaign. When the 54th marched through Boston on May 28, 1863, only about forty of its thousand men claimed Boston as their home.

The struggle for equality continued on other fronts during the war, most notably in the fight for equal pay. In that struggle, people steeped in the tradition of petition and protest exemplified by Morris made their voices heard by refusing to take the inferior pay offered them. Their "pay strike" embarrassed the Union government and white populace, and it ultimately helped persuade whites that African Americans viewed the principle of equality as non-negotiable. By 1864, black soldiers earned the same pay as white soldiers. Other black soldiers, who insisted on equality but had less experience negotiating with official power, simply stacked their arms. Convicted of mutiny, some were executed by their own government for demanding equality.

By 1864, even the old colonizationist Abraham Lincoln had been won over to the idea that black soldiers represented not only a force against the Confederacy and slavery, but an embodiment of the principles for which he wanted the reconstituted nation to stand. Encouraging the governor of Union-occupied Louisiana to consider voting rights for at least some black men, he imagined them for the first time as people with a future in America, as brethren and members of a common national household: "They would probably help," he wrote, "in some trying time to come, to keep the jewel of liberty within the family of freedom."

By the last years of the war, then, something more than emancipation was taking place. Lincoln, and with him thousands upon thousands of other white Americans, were beginning to imagine the United States as a non-racial democracy—a nation animated by a sense of common regard and common destiny. Today, this ideal is so central to our national creed that we can hardly imagine the United States without it. But it first entered our national life during the Civil War—not because of Lincoln's Proclamation, or even because of Union victory, but because free black Northern activists invented it, insisted upon it, recruited whites to the struggle for it, and made it central to the war's conduct and meaning.

Panel I Discussion

Following the presentations in Panel I: Emancipation and its Limits, panelists Scott Nelson, Edward L. Ayers, Thavolia Glymph, and Stephen Kantrowitz further discussed the topics.

Scott Reynolds Nelson: I just want to say that one of the most impressive things for me with all three of these scholars is that if you read a standard history of the American Civil War you have this image of Confederate troops moving through Confederate territory and having the widespread support of white Confederates. You have this image of black slaves hungering for access to Union armies. I think that what we see here is actually much more a story of chaos. We see a story of not just a battle that is taking place at Gettysburg, not just a battle that is taking place at Fort Wagner, but a battle that is taking place in the house. I wanted to start with Stephen. We think of the war as being from 1861 to 1865. We think of escape as something that happens in 1861. In a way, your story is that escape as a de-stabilizing force is something that starts in 1837, or even 1775, and that one of the gathering points for this controversy is outside of the South. Indeed, it is quite outside of the South.

Stephen Kantrowitz: The constant small flow of fugitives from slave states, which in 1820 include New York, to places where there is no slave code, and their establishment of themselves as individuals, as families, and as communities enmeshed in communities of free black people creates networks of solidarity that then lead people to be willing to defy federal authority. What that means is that the terms of black citizenship are not simply in the realm of the federal constitution or state constitutions, but actually in the hands of African Americans themselves. They are redefining their relationship to the body politic and to the society by refusing to accept that they are persons held to labor, by others agreeing that they should not be so, and by being willing to violate the law in order to accomplish that. It is a critical dynamic in this history.

Scott Reynolds Nelson: In a way, that dynamic brings us a civil war because Southern states feel that the North is violating the Fugitive Slave Act.

Stephen Kantrowitz: If you read the South Carolina Declaration of Immediate Causes, what it's really saying is that Northern states allowed an abolition movement to get going; they passed all these personal liberty laws impeding the return of fugitives; they are making the Southern system unsafe by encouraging people to flee it, by allowing people to talk about how bad it is, and by refusing to let Southerners recapture their slaves who go. All three of those movements—of fugitives, of their safety in the North for legal or other reasons, and of their attack against slavery as an evil—all of those things are spearheaded by free black people in the North.

Edward L. Ayers: As Virginia is deciding whether to follow South Carolina into secession, it takes months for them to debate and talk for 3,000 pages about what they are going to do. They are now left alone with North Carolina, Tennessee, and maybe Kentucky in the legislature of the United States, powerless to stop this cancer from growing. And they are right on the border.

Anthony Burns, as Steve showed with the storming of the Boston courthouse, is brought to Lumpkin's Jail in Richmond. So, they have seen not only John Brown's raid and all of these things, but Virginia is desperately trying to decide what to do. These are very real issues that have been going on for decades.

Scott Reynolds Nelson: Thavolia talked about becoming a refugee, about getting away, which is not something people learn in 1861. It is something that has a much longer and more complex history. We have Ed's story about ways that the army directly and formally interacts. There is this line in a Faulkner story, quite far away from the war, where two boys have built a sand model of the Battle of Shiloh and they're replaying what they have heard about the battle. A black man walks up who is techincally a servant, but recognizes that the world is changing, and he kicks it and says, "There's your Shiloh." This makes me think about your work, Thavolia, and the Cameron Plantation and these other places that are not formally in the war in the sense that there are not necessarily troops moving through them, but where the battlefront is kind of in the house. Can you tell us a little bit about that?

Thavolia Glymph: To go back to Steve's comments and others', it seems to me that we do ourselves a disservice when we separate the two. The plantation had always been a site of warfare from the plantation house to the fields growing cotton, sugarcane, etc. In terms of slaves running away, when black women and children and men ran away during the Civil War, they knew that the Confederacy considered them to be in flagrant rebellion. That had not changed. When Secretary Seddon and President Davis of the Confederacy met, they said, to paraphrase, "Let us make this very clear—Not only if you run away to join the Union army, but if you run away regardless, you are in flagrant rebellion of the laws of the slave South. If you give information to the Union army, you are in flagrant rebellion." So there is this long history of slaves being in flagrant rebellion, but the war opens up this totally new space for them to act out this rebellion. They are not running to the North. Northerners have a big concern that they might, but they are not. They are running to Union lines or to the swamps, which historically have provided a site of refuge. They do not expect Northerners who come down to treat them badly. They expect that they will be granted asylum and protection, that the North is just totally insane to insist that the war has nothing to do with them. It has everything to do with them, and they proved it long before the war began and they continue to prove it. Every slave that picks up and leaves is one less slave the Confederacy has to grow the crops, or to build fortifications, etc. I think that the home front and the warfront are so inextricably intertwined that we cannot separate them, and to do so is really just to muddy the waters even more.

Edward L. Ayers: I would just add that during the war, a lot of those large dots are runaway slave ads that they still continue to run in the newspapers during the war. So the white South is not acting as though there are only four years until slavery is over. They are expecting this to be reconstituted. They keep buying slaves all the way into 1864, maybe 1865. I have never looked. But they certainly spend their money on runaway slave ads, thinking that the enforcement machinery, the solidarity among white Southerners, is going to be adequate to return them.

Thavolia Glymph: The slaves never assume, even after the Proclamation, that freedom is coming. They cannot look back as we can and see that it came. One of the big stories in my work is of slave women who lead rebellions, and some of these rebellions are at the end of the war. You wonder what they are doing because the war is almost over; this is two weeks from when it will be over. Well, they did not know that it would be over in two weeks. All they knew is that the Confederate scouts were everywhere around them, and the only way they could see to make themselves and their children free was to pick up arms and help the Union army along.

Stephen Kantrowitz: I focused my remarks on the idea that freedom is not enough and something more is required for a fuller sense of belonging within the American republic. It is also the case, however, that freedom is a question mark. Up until 1865, freedom is always contingent and tentative because at any moment even a person born in freedom could be seized under the Fugitive Slave Law. Or, they could be pulled into the vortex of civil war and find themselves enslaved, as the free black Pennsylvanians rounded up by Confederate cavalry at Gettysburg learned. So the contingency of freedom is such a powerful dynamic in African-American life, both North and South throughout this period.

Scott Reynolds Nelson: Ed, I wonder if you could talk about the ways in which planters and large slave-owners, particularly in South Carolina and along the Mississippi River, are coping with the presence of Union forces. As we saw on *Visualizing Emancipation*, lots of people end up in Texas who had never been in Texas before as this migration is happening. Lots of people end up in upcountry South Carolina who had been in low country South Carolina.

Edward L. Ayers: A lot of people end up in Richmond who had not been there before as well. I am going to answer your question, but I am going to bring it back to Virginia and Edmund Ruffin, who everyone will remember was sent down to South Carolina to fire the first shot. In 1862, he is writing from his plantation not far from here, saying, "We can hardly believe the speed with which the servants are absconding." He admits in his own diary, to paraphrase: "We just never thought that after we had told ourselves that they were part of our families, that they loved us, we loved them, we worshipped together—that they would abscond, or steal themselves, instantly." People look around and say, "You better get the heck out of Dodge and ship your slaves. You better escape yourself as a white refugee." That is what I am saying, Richmond triples in size over the course of the war with refugees. Others, if they have the means, are taking their enslaved property to where they think the war will never come. To Texas or to—ironically, if you had gone to Mississippi you would have been safe most of the time. So, there is that profound dislocation as well. I was emphasizing the uncertainty and the churn among the lives of white and black. Part of it too, is people are completely uprooting from where they have lived their entire lives and moving to other places.

Scott Reynolds Nelson: I love the phrase "Confederate men in the shade" while others are building fortifications. We think about conscription as being something that happens in 1862, but of course slaves are conscripted by the Confederacy in April of 1861. The first conscripts, really, are slaves. We think about the Confederates preserving slavery, but in a way they are de-stabilizing it.

Edward L. Ayers: It is not as if the slave-owners are happy about this, thinking, "Confederate government, come take away my largest and most powerful men and put them to work where they may certainly be injured and very well die digging in the malarial swamps on the peninsula. And they are going down there beyond my vision or an overseer—and you are giving me how much?"

One thing we point out is that enslaved people had never been worth more to their masters than in 1860. The war comes at the very time that masters and mistresses had been acquiring a large increase in the value of their property. Now the Confederate government, which had existed for all of six months by this time, comes in and says, "Give us your slaves and we may give them back. We will give you a few dollars on it." Of course, everyone recognizes the irony of having states' rights so that you do not have a strong federal government. It becomes a horrific experience for the enslaved people themselves.

Scott Reynolds Nelson: Thavolia, besides ex-slave narratives, one of the things that you use a lot are plantation diaries, including John Tyler and others. Slaveholders want to know what this Confederacy business is. The government is taking ten percent of their slaves and then the slaves are dying. The world as the slaveholders have built it is collapsing.

Thavolia Glymph: As you will hear this afternoon, this is the subject of Stephanie McCurry's important book *Confederate Reckoning*. At the very moment that the Confederate states decide to secede and establish this confederacy, they doomed themselves. In their diaries and letters, slaveholders seem so surprised when slaves leave. However, at the same time, it seems quite interesting to me that they are at once surprised and not. They will say, "Oh, Joe and Mandy went off this morning and, God forbid, they are going to die because they cannot survive without us." Then the next sentence will say, "What will *I* do without them?" It is a recognition of the slaves' politics, their humanity and their contributions to the plantation South even when slaveholders continue to mouth the conceit that slaves should have stayed because they are part of the family, which is the big joke. As we know, some twelve percent of the slave population walks off. That is not an insignificant number in terms of the financial investment of the South. I read these things with a sense that slaveholders are really not surprised. In South Carolina planters flee when the combined amphibious expedition of the Union army and navy lands at Hilton Head in November 1861. Within weeks, we find them asking, "Is it safe to go back? Joe's family refused to even come with us. Can we go back and force them to come?" They are acknowledging that their hold on enslaved people is very tenuous. They cannot go back themselves and get them and the slaves will not come voluntarily to the upcountry where the planters have taken refuge.

Scott Reynolds Nelson: I am reminded of this line from W.E.B. DuBois, something like, "The vagabonds who arrive at the camps in their dark despair." In 1903, DuBois has a story about the side of the Freedmen's Bureau that we do not see, which is the terrible humanitarian crisis. What are some of the problems people face in contraband camps?

Thavolia Glymph: It depends. If you are in a contraband camp in Hampton, Virginia or Alexandria, you are in a pretty settled community with fairly well-constructed housing where a number of Northerners have come to help. If you are in the Mississippi Valley, you are in a shack or on an abandoned plantation where both armies are actively leveling everything and Confederate forces are burning and destroying refugee camps, many of which have become staging grounds from which the Union army and the Treasury Department secure workers. When the treasury takes over these plantations, they need people to work them and grow more cotton. So, they pull women and children from the refugee camps and place them in the labor camps where they are vulnerable to Confederate military attacks. Here the Federal government places inexperienced black soldiers who had just been recruited from the camps themselves to protect the camps, and they often are no match for Confederate cavalry or artillery. It is a pretty dismal situation.

Scott Reynolds Nelson: That use of what is essentially uncompensated labor is a big part of how the Union occupation works.

Edward L. Ayers: It is easy to idealize the small dots and the large dots. One of the possible entries is "conscription," which means that slaves have to go at that moment, no matter if their family needs them or not. They are now part of the Union army. They cannot say that it isn't a good time or that it is unjust—they do not have that choice. I think we need to recognize that there was an element of enforcement involved. One thing that we know about all home fronts is that all food is remarkably perishable. Just imagine if you do not have any canning, any freezers, or any CARE packages being dropped into these camps. The food is walking around on four legs. One of the first things that any army does is kill the livestock, take it, and drag it away. As we imagine what the landscape for survival for both white and black would be, it is just devastated by that necessity. One of the worst things that could happen to many people was that the Union army arrives because though they might be a vehicle for your freedom, one thing is for certain: they are going to take the fences down and kill the hogs. I want to make sure that I do not make that very clean-looking map seem schematic. This was desperate from start to finish.

Stephen Kantrowitz: At least until the Emancipation Proclamation, and, in reality, into 1864 and even 1865, what it means for an enslaved person to encounter the Union is anybody's guess. In the aggregate, the hypothesis that the Union is going to provide some form of sanctuary turns out to work enough of the time that people continue to move toward the Union.

Edward L. Ayers: Toward the risk.

Stephen Kantrowitz: Exactly, because it is not slavery—mostly. That does not mean that at the fine-grained level people's experiences were anything like that all the time.

Edward L. Ayers: We started looking at the runaway slave ads in Richmond in the early 1860s and they say, "Went to the army." This is before the Union army was there. This means that they are running away to the Confederacy. What they are really running away to is: A) It is not slavery. B) I can earn some money of my own. C) I might be able to bring my family there. In the same way that having an army there, blue or gray, might be good or bad, it might also be a way to pry yourself away from the plantation as well.

Scott Reynolds Nelson: There are many destinies in these refugee camps. The African Americans who are following Sherman's army are left behind, in many cases with bridges destroyed to prevent them from following. There is no way, with our kinds of sources, to tell that story. We know that there are many casualties, but they are not casualties on the battlefield of Gettysburg. They are casualties ten miles behind the lines.

Edward L. Ayers: Or drowning in the swamps.

Thavolia Glymph: We cannot tell it completely, but I am convinced that we can tell it better than we have, in part because the federal government was involved and any time you have government involved, you have records. Just as we have these wonderful Freedmen's Bureau records, we also have a pre-Freedmen's Bureau, the Freedmen's Department. The Freedmen's Department brought doctors into the camps. The treasury agents went into the camps with a census form, and that census form has the name of the now-freed person, his age, sex, color—black, mulatto, whatever—the plantation from which he or she fled, sometimes height, and where they were born.

When I see that in a camp there are ten people who were born in Virginia, then I know immediately that these ten people have made that pre-war migration to the new southwest and the new cotton fields. Now they are undergoing a second migration. Taking the census records from the Treasury Department, the War Department, and the Freedmen's Department and trying to locate those people in the 1870 census, you can see how many people survived from a particular camp and where they went. I have all of these women and children who are in this camp in the Valley in 1864 and I know their ages and where they were born. In 1870, five of these women are now in Kansas and I wonder how they got there. You can determine that between 1863 and 1870 they have had children. Or maybe a child that was with them in 1864 is no longer with them and perhaps has died.

Edward L. Ayers: If you look at *Visualizing Emancipation*, there are hundreds of instances where the Union army is a federal agency. They say, "Yikes, I have all of these women here to feed." Or, "Hooray." It depends on if you are trying to move or if you are a stable army. The point is, as the Union army is moving, it has to wrestle with this issue of women coming to camp and what to do with them.

Scott Reynolds Nelson: What does the emancipation equation look like for African Americans? What are the other things that you are thinking about besides freedom? There's an equation of deciding to fight, to leave, or to stay. Where do you put yourself in relation to this conflict?

Thavolia Glymph: I think Ed's mapping project shows that it is a complicated decision. Maybe you stay because the Union army has come and that makes it a safer space. Maybe you stay because in your particular area there is a community where you can build a different kind of society because masters have fled. You leave because you decide that freedom is more likely, more available within Union lines than on this plantation where you are. I think it's very complicated and these are at once individual decisions but also community decisions because you may decide you want to follow your husband, whether he has been coerced into or volunteered to join the Union or pulled into the Confederate military operation as a conscripted laborer. A lot of the cases are women and children who follow their husbands and fathers to Union camps and the Union commanders turn them away. Even after the Emancipation Proclamation, after the First Confiscation Act, the Second Confiscation Act, the Militia Act, they still continue to put these women and children beyond the bounds of Union lines to fend for themselves. This is where you get these makeshift camps.

Ed, you made a reference to Sherman. The army commanders see themselves as having a job to do, and that job is to win this war on the battlefield. The battlefields that they have in mind do not have women and children on them. Sherman comes through and says to his commanders, "We cannot have that baggage."

That is, the women, children, and slaves following them. When his commanders get to Savannah and file their reports, they tell Sherman that they followed instructions. "I had twenty following me"—or, more likely, five hundred following me—"and of that five hundred, when I got to Savannah, there were ten." Usually those ten were people they could incorporate into the army as workers. A lot of people were left behind in the swamps when they pulled the pontoon bridges up. They were left behind to Confederate raiders who could not get to Sherman's men, but could pick off the slaves who were following them. When you read the Confederate side of the Atlanta campaign, the Confederate commanders are saying, "I found two hundred here and I returned them to slavery."

Stephen Kantrowitz: The two big dimensions are local knowledge and national politics. Local knowledge, especially before 1863, is really critical because some commanders are going to welcome contraband into their camps and some are not. Some are going to exclude them or allow slaveholders to recapture them, whether or not those slaveholders can profess loyalty to the Union. The networks of rumor and information that travel among slaves are really important for determining where it makes sense to go and where it does not. Where is a reasonable risk and where is not? The local knowledge really matters.

On the national timescale, by 1863 when the Union moves to a policy of active conscription of slaves into the service as soldiers, things change a lot because the Union is not going to return slaves to their owners as a matter of policy. It is not even going to allow loyal slaveholders to reclaim their slave property, even in Kentucky by 1863 or 1864. We get to a moment where the local knowledge shifts to a much more general knowledge, and in that moment, especially when slaves run into Union encampments, there is a critical encounter between slaves and black soldiers.

Edward L. Ayers: Let us pull the camera back even more. None of this happens without secession. The process of emancipation starts with the individual states breaking apart and then the Confederate government forming. One way to think about this is that if this campaign to take Richmond in 1862 had succeeded and the war had ended then, then slavery would not have ended as it did. Douglass says, "Once let the black man get upon his person the brass letter, U.S., let him get an eagle on his button, and a musket on his shoulder and bullets in his pocket, there is no power on earth that can deny that he has earned the right to citizenship." You could also say, "Let them get a taste of freedom, you cannot put it back in the bottle." Where did emancipation come from? In many ways, it comes from the Confederate states themselves, from the white Southerners who vote for these delegates and then secession. It also comes from the Confederate army fighting long enough to force the United States to make anti-slavery a war aim.

Stephen Kantrowitz: You are suggesting that it is not only as DuBois said, "When Edmund Ruffin, white-haired and mad, fired the first gun at Fort Sumter, he freed the slaves." It is also the failure of George McClellan.

Edward L. Ayers: You could even say that if Virginia had not decided to join this new Confederacy in April 1861, the course of slavery would have been different and therefore the war would have been different. Steve used my favorite word of "contingency" about all of this on the local level. It is also on the very largest level. From my perspective, that restores a huge element of the drama of all of this. Sometimes the home front feels like a history without an event, without shape that is just privation and hope and waiting for the letter home saying that your son has been killed. Life on the home front, especially if you are held in bondage, has a shape and a history that we are just beginning to piece together.

Thavolia Glymph: We have to remember that when Lincoln went to the border states and begged them to go along with compensated emancipation, he tells them, "This is our chance for you to get your money for these people, and if you do not take it now, the war will be beyond us." This is when he uses all of that wonderful phrasing about friction.

Scott Reynolds Nelson: "Friction and abrasion."

Thavolia Glymph: The same thing happens in September 1862 with the Preliminary Proclamation when he says, "You have one hundred days to do this, and if you do not, then I am going to free your slaves."

Stephen Kantrowitz: We talk a lot about Lincoln's plans for compensation for slaveholders who were willing to free their slaves. Compensation, compensation, compensation. At no point does the national conversation during the Civil War shift to compensation for the former slaves, to freedom dues, which are what apprentices get when they come out of their servitude. There is no sustained national conversation about freedom dues or compensation to the slaves for their unrequited toil.

Confederate Reckoning: The People and Their Politics On The Home Front

Stephanie McCurry

If we want to grapple seriously with the Confederate home front and the state it was in by 1863, we have to begin by asking what the Confederate project was—what kind of republic white Southerners intended to build when they seceded from the Union—because the problem of democratic consent (of carrying the support of the people for war) was there from the beginning. It was inherent in the very limited idea of "the people" as it was defined in the slaveholders' new republic. After the war was over Confederate leaders would say that they simply wanted to restore the republic as it was originally intended to be, that there was nothing revolutionary about their goals. By that point, however, they were attempting to obscure the principles—the explicitly proslavery principles—that drove their movement for national independence. It might seem harsh, but there is no other way to put it. What secessionists set out to do was something entirely new in the history of nations: to build an explicitly proslavery and anti-democratic nation state, a country dedicated to the principle that all men were NOT created equal.

As we know, it would not work out that way. Their gamble on the future of slavery instead brought down the largest slaveholding regime in the western world. Still, that was their intention: to build a government explicitly pledged to the enslavement of black people into perpetuity and to the permanent limitation of the vote to white men. The Confederacy was to be a country that defended slavery, rejected democracy, and scorned the Declaration of Independence. Secession was a huge gamble and it was a gamble on the future of slavery. In Virginia, especially, the limitations of the Confederacy's view of democracy made many white men uneasy. From here in the Upper South, men in 1861 looked down on the secession of the Deep South states with incredible suspicion. They didn't trust the big slaveholders there or, for that matter, in the eastern parts of their own state.

But the crisis of democracy in the new Confederacy did not end with secession. Indeed, to me, the Confederacy is as much a story of political failure as military defeat.

Something that has not really been noticed is that the Confederacy was based on a very slim foundation of democratic consent. Secessionists claimed the consent of "the people" (as they had to), but it is important to remember what that meant in slave republics in the nineteenth century. It meant white men. Around 1.5 million Southerners out of a total population of 10 million (that is to say, the number of white male voters) were ever consulted about the wisdom of secession and war. But if it took only 1.5 million to create the republic, it would have taken all 10 million to defend it in war.

When we remember that so many non-slaveholding whites were opposed to secession to start with, we start to grasp the problem. Add to that what we have learned about the actions of enslaved people in the history of the Civil War and emancipation, which is that as much as Confederates refused (or were unable) to think of slaves as part of the people, slaves' politics mattered and the actions they took to destroy slavery and the slaveholders' republic were fundamental in its defeat.

We must also think of the other huge population of Southerners excluded and disfranchised—white women, most of them from non-slaveholding families. In 1861, nobody cared about their views or bothered to ask whether they supported secession or if they were open to the risks of war. By 1863, it was a different matter, and the Confederate project was subject to the judgment of its own people—all of its own people—including the women. This is what I mean by "the Reckoning."

If we think about it, the problem is obvious and it has to do with the peculiarities of a slave regime at war. The Confederacy had an economy and a population a fraction the size of its enemy. The South's population of ten million was dwarfed by the Union's twenty-two million, but even that understates the problem because forty percent of adult men in the South were enslaved and thus unavailable for military service. It was as if it had a population of only six million in fact.

It quickly became clear what those kinds of imbalances meant. The South had to exert insupportable demands on its people and take measures drastic even by standards of the North. It was forced to impress slaves, for example, which posed tests of nationalism many slaveholders failed.

Of course, after only one year of war, the Davis administration was driven to adopt the first conscription act in American history. The Confederacy was forced to mobilize a far higher proportion of white men than the United States. When all was said and done, a staggering seventy-five to eighty-five percent of white men served in the Confederate military (compared to fifty percent in the North). When combined with exemptions that the government was forced to make for slaveholders—the famous twenty-Negro law—conscription quickly raised cries of "rich man's war, poor man's fight."

But it was women's fight as well. What does a home front look like with eighty-five percent of the men gone? The countryside was, as the women put it, "stripped of men." It became women's domain.

The South was an agrarian society, whole regions of it populated by yeoman and poor white families. There had never been any expectation that women could make subsistence on those farms without the labor of men. And indeed they could not. By 1863, with husbands and sons in the war, the food crisis in the Confederacy reached starvation proportions. It then turned into a political crisis provoked by women trying to force the government to fulfill its promises to support them—promises made when it took their men. The politics of subsistence, and the mass of Confederate soldiers' wives who made it so, was one entirely unanticipated element of reckoning war had brought.

As it turns out, the Confederacy faced a daunting political challenge from the mass of white Southern women in their new collective identity as "soldiers' wives." The Confederate government had created them and would now have to answer to them. The evidence of women's agitation and activism is all over the place, in the thousands of letters and petitions written to government officials to try to get their men out of the service and in the way they deluged politicians with warnings about the consequences of a military policy geared toward the interests of the "big men," as they often put it. Sometimes they were just begging letters, but often the communications were angry, threatening. Speaking in a collective voice—"We Soldiers' Wives"—they demanded not just relief but

Northern View of the Southern Bread Riots, *Frank Leslie's Illustrated Newspaper*, May 1863.

justice for the Confederate poor. All this evidence is in the archives, where it has been missed for generations.

But nobody missed what happened next. In the spring of 1863, soldiers' wives took to the streets in protest, in a wave of food riots that hit the South from Mobile, Alabama to Richmond, Virginia. Then, mobs of women numbering from a dozen to more than three hundred and armed with navy revolvers, bowie knives and hatchets, carried out at least twelve violent attacks on stores, government warehouses, army convoys, railroad depots, saltworks, and granaries. The attacks occurred in broad daylight, and were all perpetrated in the space of one month, between the middle of March and the middle of April 1863.

Needless to say, conspiracy theories abounded. "This must be the work of men, Yankee agents." In most cases we do not know how the riots were organized, but in Richmond, the largest of the riots, we do. As it turns out, it was not the work of men but of one Mary Jackson: soldier's mother, farm wife, and huckster in meat at the public market. She had tried appealing to the Secretary of War to release her son—hers just one of the thousands of angry, threatening, barely literate letters written by soldiers' wives and mothers to officials over the course of the war. The riots, in other words, were just the tip of the iceberg—the part we see.

Most women never crossed the line to violence. But when Mary Jackson got no satisfaction, she recruited three hundred town and country women to a meeting at the Belvidere Baptist Church, got up into the pulpit to rally her troops (already a violation of every gender code), told them to gather the next morning at the entrance to Capitol Square, to leave their children at home, and to come armed. It was truly a Confederate Spring of soldiers' wives discontent. The next morning they met as planned, demanded a meeting with the governor, and, when they didn't get it, took to the streets where they rampaged for hours. The rioters were brought under control only when state militia was called out and ordered to fire upon them.

At the end, the whole lot of them were rounded up and arrested, captured all over the working-class districts of the city, sitting on their hauls of stolen goods. It was their trial that left us the record. Mary Jackson was arrested around noon, wearing two pistols on her hips and yelling, allegedly, "bread or blood," the slogan that had emerged in Mobile and was used in many of the riots.

Confederate women had been totally excluded from the processes of democratic consent by which the Confederacy was founded and set on the path to war. But, as it turned out, they were part of "the people" whose consent and support mattered to the government.

The women made themselves count. The wave of food riots had a direct effect on Confederate war policy. It forced revisions of conscription and tax policy, but most importantly it forced the development of a massive welfare program by the states and even the central government, which, after the riots, wrote legislation allocating scarce funds and foodstuffs to the relief of women and children. In the heart of Confederate territory, the mass of white Southern women had emerged as formidable adversaries or critics of the government in the long struggle over the justice of its military policies. By insisting that the government live up to its promises to protect them, these poor white women, who had never participated in politics before, stepped decisively into the making of history.

The new political assertiveness of Southern women did not bring down the Confederacy, but it did represent a powerful challenge to the original Confederate vision of the people and the republic. It also showed the limitations of their proslavery and antidemocratic nationalism. Even as the Confederacy attempted to survive the brutal military test posed by the Union armies, even as it had to expend scarce men and military resources to put down the constant insurrection of enslaved men and women within Confederate territory, it also had to fend off the challenge that came from non-elite white women.

As they made clear, any government that took their men would ultimately have to answer to them.

The Other Emancipation: Plain Folk vs. Aristocrats in the Invaded South

Stephen V. Ash

The invasion of the Confederacy by Union armies unsettled Southern society in more ways than one. We have heard here today very interesting discussions of how black Southerners took advantage of the Union invasion to achieve emancipation. What I want to talk about this afternoon is another emancipation that took place side by side with that of the slaves: the emancipation of the South's poor white people.

The Old South was dominated socially, politically, and economically by wealthy and cultured aristocrats, most of them owners of large plantations and many slaves. Below this small but powerful elite class in the white social hierarchy was a group historians have labeled "the plain folk." Most of the plain folk were skilled tradesmen or farmers who owned small to middling size farms and herds; they lived comfortably, though certainly not opulently, and most had at least a basic education. But among the plain folk there were a substantial number of utterly propertyless men and women, unskilled, poorly educated, many wholly illiterate, who eked out a marginal living and were generally looked down upon by other whites, especially the aristocrats. It is this segment of the plain folk, the impoverished and unlettered who lived hard lives, which I speak of today.

Before the Civil War there was little evidence of serious conflict between the propertied and property-less whites of the South. But resentment of the rich by the poor and fear of the poor by the rich were always simmering below the surface. With the outbreak of war in 1861 and the subsequent invasion of many sections of the South by Union armies, these resentments and fears began to break forth into the open.

Southern elites worried that the poor whites, whom they scorned as uncouth, undisciplined, and untrustworthy because they had no property and thus had nothing to lose, would run riot in the chaos accompanying Yankee invasion. Even worse, they might ally themselves with the Yankees in the hope of sharing the spoils of war. A Confederate officer expressed this concern as a Union army advanced up the Virginia Peninsula toward Richmond in the spring of 1862. He was worried in particular about the poor whites who made a living fishing on the James River, and whom he referred to as "low white men." He feared they might volunteer to serve as guides for the Yankees and in response ordered his troops to destroy the poor whites' fishing boats. In reporting this decision to his superior, he justified it by asserting that these poor whites were "as dangerous as the negroes."

The Northern soldiers who invaded the South, and other Northerners who accompanied the Union armies, also had a role to play in the unfolding story of the South's poor whites. Decades of Northern propaganda had created in the Yankee mind a stereotype of Southern society that was, in many ways, grossly exaggerated. The South was a medieval anachronism, Northerners believed. The planter aristocracy ruled the South despotically, monopolizing wealth, power, and knowledge, and lording it over the plain folk as well as the slaves. The planters had taken the South out of the Union solely to preserve their power, and in doing so had taken advantage of the ignorance of the plain folk and ruthlessly suppressed those who protested. If these downtrodden whites could be freed from the power of the aristocrats, the Yankees believed, they would surely rally to the cause of the Union and help the North win the war.

On arriving in the South, many Yankees perceived exactly what their stereotypes had prepared them for. A Union officer in middle Tennessee in 1862 commented that "the poor whites are as poor as rot, and the rich are very rich. There is no substantial middle class here." Often the Northerners explicitly linked the poor whites with the slaves, portraying both as long-suffering victims of aristocratic tyranny. A Northern journalist in the Virginia tidewater in 1862 remarked that the poor whites he saw were "certainly as debased and degraded as the poor negroes." A Northern woman who came to an occupied town in Florida to serve as a schoolteacher for the freed slaves also took note of the poor whites: "They are miserably poor and ignorant and dirty," she said, "in many instances needing as much sympathy and help as the fugitive negro." In that town and others held by Union forces, the army provided rations for the poor whites while Northern missionaries set up schools for them just as they did for the newly freed blacks.

The poor whites themselves were not passive participants in this drama of invasion and occupation. Like the slaves, they took a leading role. In some cases they fulfilled the fears of the aristocrats by taking advantage of the disorder that accompanied the arrival of Union armies. In early 1862, as Union forces reached the outskirts of Nashville and Confederate troops hurriedly evacuated, poor whites in the city rioted, breaking into stores and warehouses and carrying off goods of every sort. Just a few weeks later, similar scenes were enacted in New Orleans as Rebel troops abandoned the city to the Yankees. Savannah, Mobile, and other Southern towns likewise witnessed poor-white rioting when the Yankees arrived.

Once the Northern invaders had established themselves securely in garrisoned towns, many poor whites in the surrounding areas made their way to these military posts to escape hardships in the countryside or to seek new opportunities. Typical of these was a day laborer who arrived at a Union post in Florida in 1862; questioned by the provost marshal, he explained that "I came to Pensacola to find work, and something to eat." Refugees like this man headed in the opposite direction from the refugees more familiar to us, that is, the white Southerners who fled from the Yankees to areas still under Confederate control. The poor whites who went to the Yankees were of course following the same paths as the many thousands of enslaved black people who slipped away from their masters and sought shelter and opportunity with the invaders.

Many poor whites in the occupied regions further fulfilled aristocratic fears by actually aiding the Yankees. In Virginia in 1862, a Union soldier engaged in seizing supplies from local farms made this observation: "There are two classes of white people in this [region]—the poor class and the wealthy or aristocratic class. The poor ones are very bitter against the others; [they] charge them with bringing on the war, and are always willing to show where the rich ones have hid their grain, fodder, horses, &c. Many of them tell me it is a great satisfaction to them to see us help ourselves from the rich stores of their neighbors." Tens of thousands of poor-white men, especially in western Virginia and Tennessee, manifested their resentment against the Southern aristocracy (as well as their Union patriotism) by enlisting in the Union army and helping to defeat the Rebel nation that the aristocrats had created.

To elite Southerners, all this evidence of poor-white restlessness, opportunism, and disaffection was not only infuriating but frightening. A Mississippi judge wrote to the state's governor in 1864 to tell him of the poor whites who were leaving the Confederate-held areas of the state and heading to the Yankee lines. They were, he said, a "filthy, base, disloyal, deserting, stealing, murdering population. . . . They ought to be hung. They pretend to go there to get corn to live on, but their real object is to avoid our army, steal, plunder, and be with the Yankees. I . . . know them to be a base, vile & worthless set who never made a good or honest living. . . . They are all as rotten as Hell."

But even scarier things were in store for the Southern aristocracy. As time passed, some poor whites boldly staked a claim to the property and power they had never possessed under the old regime, and in doing so they threatened to revolutionize Southern society as thoroughly as the black people who were bringing an end to slavery. In many areas surrounding the Yankee-held towns, poor whites seized and occupied farms and plantations that had been abandoned by families that had fled to the Confederate lines. In 1864, an alarmed Mississippian reported to the governor that "[people] from the hills are flocking in & settling all the vacant places. . . . Many of them seem to have no means of livilihood. It is also said they are harboring [Confederate] deserters." In some cases, poor whites did not wait for these homesteads to be abandoned, but simply squatted on the land, began farming it, and dared the owner to do anything about it. A planter in eastern North Carolina pleaded with Confederate authorities in 1864 to send troops to crack down on the "lawless & dollarless men" who infested his locality, which was not far from a Union-occupied town. "[S]ome of those fellows," the planter reported, "have already said they will cultivate any mans land they please."

A place in the middle Tennessee highlands known as Beersheba Springs experienced what can only be called a poor-white uprising. Beersheba was a resort where wealthy Southerners gathered for extended summer vacations, living in the elegant hotel or the lavishly furnished private cottages. Despite the Yankee military occupation of Tennessee and the disruption that accompanied it, a number of aristocratic families gathered at Beersheba as usual in the summer of 1863, confident that they would be safe. But on a day in late July they learned otherwise, as a mob of local inhabitants whom the resort guests condescendingly referred to as the "mountain people" suddenly descended on the place.

A woman named Virginia French, who was summering in one of the cottages, described in her diary what happened: "Scenes enacted here today beggar description," she wrote. "Early in the morning the sack of the place began. . . . [T]he mountain people came in crowds and with vehickles of all sorts and carried off everything they could from both hotel and cottages. . . . Gaunt, ill-looking men and slatternly, rough barefooted women stalking and racing to and fro, eager as famished wolves for prey, hauling out furniture. . . . A band would rush up and take possession of a cottage—place a guard, [and] drive off every one else, stating that this was theirs." French noted in particular one woman who emerged from a cottage carrying a stack of books on theology, Latin, and French. "The woman, who did not know a letter [of the alphabet] to save her life, said 'she had some children who were just beginin' to read and . . . she wanted to encourage 'em!'" To French it seemed like a world turned upside down: "[T]he masses' had it all their own way on this memorable day,—the aristocrats went down for the nonce, and Democracy—Jacobinism—and Radicalism in their rudest forms reigned triumphant." The "mountain people" returned the next day for more plundering, and several more times before the summer ended.

Aristocrats in the occupied South were further dismayed to learn that the Yankee invaders, or some of them at least, were anxious to lend a hand in turning Southern society topsy-turvy.

"The more we learn of the despicable social condition of the South," declared a Northern soldier in eastern North Carolina in 1863, "the stronger appears the need of the purification which, in the Providence of God, comes of the fire and the sword." The destruction of slavery was one aspect of this purification; raising up the poor whites and bringing down the aristocracy were also part of the plan. In 1864 a Nashville newspaper published under federal authority called on the poor to cast off their chains and create a more just and equitable society: "Non-slaveholders of Tennessee," the paper asked rhetorically, "what have [you] to gain by longer remaining subservient to a heartless, domineering aristocracy[?]" In Nashville and other occupied towns in Tennessee, Louisiana, Virginia, and elsewhere, poor whites flocked to political rallies organized by the Yankees as a first step toward reconstructing the Southern state governments on a more egalitarian basis.

By 1864 it seemed to some observers that poor-white insurgency—abetted by the Yankees—might well bring about a radical transformation of white society in the occupied South. However, there were powerful countervailing forces at work that impeded the revolutionary momentum.

One was racism. Many poor whites regarded aristocrats not as enemies, but as allies in the struggle to keep the black population under control. Few poor whites welcomed the destruction of slavery, for the existence of a subjugated class of black people had always provided poor whites, however miserable their own circumstances, with the ideological satisfaction of membership in a superior class.

Many aristocrats in the occupied South were gratified to see evidence of poor-white racial solidarity. In southeastern Virginia, for example, in the summer of 1862, a party of poor whites ambushed a group of runaway slaves, killed one of them, and returned another to his owner—a deed that one aristocrat praised as "commendable." Many Yankees, naively assuming that the poor whites and slaves were natural allies of one another in the struggle to overthrow the Southern aristocracy, were disappointed to find that the poor whites did not see it that way at all. One Northerner described a conversation he had with a poor-white woman in Mississippi concerning the causes of the war. The woman, who told the Northerner she had never owned a slave in her life and never expected to, insisted that the war was all the North's fault. "We-uns didn't want to fight, no-how," she said. "You-uns went and made the war so as to steal our [Negroes]."

Another factor limiting the revolutionary momentum in the occupied South was the attitude of many of the Yankee occupiers. Not all Northerners sympathized with the poor whites and wanted to empower them, and some who did changed their minds after being in the South for a time. Some, in fact, grew so disgusted with the poor whites' bitter racism and their refusal to conform to middle-class Yankee notions of propriety that they abandoned all hope of enlisting them in the effort to transform the South. As a Union officer in South Carolina in 1865 expressed it, the poor whites were "lower than the negro in every respect, [including] general intelligence, culture and morality. . . . They are not fit to be kept in the same sty with a well to do farmer's hogs in New England." A Northern journalist in Savannah agreed: the poor whites, he wrote, are "far below the colored people in ability and force of character. They are a class from which there is little to hope."

A third factor was the powerful counteroffensive mounted by the Southern elite as soon as the war ended. With the defeat of the Confederate armies in the spring of 1865, President Andrew Johnson began withdrawing Union military forces from the South and initiated a generous policy of amnesty and pardon toward the defeated Rebels. This policy allowed aristocrats to resume the positions of authority they had customarily monopolized. Armed with local and state governmental power, aristocrats moved forcefully against the poor whites who had challenged them during the war.

In September 1865 a Northern journalist in Virginia interviewed an official of the Spotsylvania County court. This gentleman was full of complaints about the current situation in Spotsylvania, but his chief grievance was the Union army's policy of feeding the indigent poor whites. "The system encourages idleness," he said, "and does more harm than good." These whites were "shiftless," he explained, "steeped in vice, ignorance, and crime of every description. They have no comforts, and no energy to work and obtain them. They have no books, no morality, no religion; they go [about] clothed like savages." If the army occupation force was gone, he told the journalist, the county court could deal with these miscreants as they deserved. About that same time, in Pointe Coupee Parish, Louisiana, the local authorities sternly ordered the squatters who had taken over abandoned lands during the war to vacate those lands immediately, adding that if the squatters resisted they would feel the full power of the law.

Similar scenes were enacted across the South in the postwar months. Meanwhile, Southern elites were also moving forcefully to rein in the emancipated slaves. This did not mean, however, that the social upheaval triggered by the Union invasion of the South was at an end. Black people were determined to expand the boundaries of their freedom, while many poor whites remained hopeful of claiming a greater share of wealth and power. Both groups would find a powerful ally in the US Congress, which by the end of 1865 had decided that President Johnson's policies must not prevail.

Thus the stage was set for the momentous struggles of the Reconstruction era. But that's another story.

What Did Good Citizenship Mean during the Civil War?

J. Matthew Gallman

Students of Civil War dissent are perhaps too quick to think of the North in simple binary terms, where the "Copperheads" opposed the war and everyone else was fundamentally part of a homogeneous pro-war group. The first part is pretty accurate: there were antiwar Democrats, known as Copperheads, who actively opposed the war and the Lincoln administration, some of whom would have been happy to see the administration toppled. But there were also large numbers of Northerners who remained in favor of the war while also engaging in active dissent, both from the left and the right of the political spectrum. Outside the bounds of normal partisan disagreement, the North witnessed fairly substantial conflict and dissent—and occasional violence—from citizens who objected to the draft and from wage-earning workers who faced declining real wages. In short, during the war years the Union saw much more conflict, disagreement, and uncertainty than we commonly recognize. And, in truth, when we consider the vast scale of that conflict and its ambiguous end point, we should not be surprised that Abraham Lincoln and his administration endured quite a bit of loyal grumbling in addition to the open disloyalty displayed by the Copperheads.

This idea that the Civil War produced uncertainty, as well as angry dissent, deserves further scrutiny. The majority of Northerners supported the war effort, but a large share of those fundamentally "patriotic" Americans did so with no clear sense of how they should act in the midst of a huge civil war. Consider two simple, and seemingly contradictory, observations. First, Americans had no familiarity with a war that approached the scale of the American Civil War. The size of the armies, the demands on the economy, and the long casualty lists published in newspapers across the country all outstripped any prior experiences. The past offered no clear roadmap for how individual citizens should respond. Second, although the armies were huge and the nation's hardships were real, many Northerners lived through four years of war without experiencing any personal danger or economic hardship. Large numbers of military-aged men declined to enlist, and the combined weight of a state militia draft and four federal conscriptions only produced a relatively small number of unwilling conscripts. The North faced substantial inflation (although negligible compared with what the Confederacy endured), but the war-heated economy boomed, unemployment nearly disappeared, and there were no crippling war-related shortages. For many, in material terms, life went on even as reports from the battlefield kept arriving.

Those Northerners who supported the war but who were not compelled by circumstances to sacrifice for the cause found themselves with a series of decisions about how they should respond. For some, this was hardly a question at all. As soon as the president called for volunteers, thousands of young men raced to the nearest recruiting station, while many women and older men immediately threw themselves into voluntary efforts to assist the war effort. But while these citizens perhaps saw matters with great clarity, the war presented most Northerners with complex decisions about how they should behave and also about how they should judge the actions of others. It is my contention (and what follows draws on material in a forthcoming book) that Northerners responded to the unfamiliar challenges of the Civil War much as antebellum Americans had wrestled with the myriad economic and cultural challenges of the previous decades: they turned to a diverse world of published materials that offered advice, guidance, and cautionary tales to anxious readers hoping to find clues about how to navigate the unfamiliar.

Some of the most pointed messages came in the form of cartoons and satirical writings which collectively mapped out a world of the unsavory, the hypocritical, and the grossly selfish, all of whom—in these caricatured forms—had found ways to profit from the war's opportunities while skirting its obligations. *Frank Leslie's Budget of Fun*, a popular comic monthly, ran a cartoon called "Precept and Practice" lampooning the hypocrisy of the patriotic press. In the first frame, a prowar editor is congratulating himself for his latest editorial, attacking "the man who hesitates to give his life for his country in crisis." In the second frame – "Practice"—the same man has learned that he has been visited by "the Conscription Man," prompting him to rush out the back door and head for Canada.

"Precept and Practice," from *Frank Leslie's Budget of Fun*, June 1863.

"Some of the Shoddy Aristocracy," a cartoon in *Harper's New Monthly Magazine*, featured three pairs of images. The first in each pair shows a humble retailer plying his or her trade in 1860, while the second portrays the same person in 1863, bloated with ill-gotten wealth, having made a fortune selling "shoddy" goods to wartime consumers.

These two cartoons and hundreds more produced during the war poked fun at the dishonest and the hypocritical. Collectively, this world of subtle humor and biting satire identified for ordinary citizens who the war's true villains were. Meanwhile, wartime fiction—not unlike antebellum writing—commonly offered readers prescriptive messages about the disasters that awaited characters who behaved badly during the war. In the process, the

"Some of the Shoddy Aristocracy," from *Harper's New Monthly Magazine*, September 1863.

cultural messages served to reassure everyone else that their own wartime foibles were probably not so bad.

If a large portion of wartime popular culture served to identify behavior that society should reject, quite a bit of the rest aimed to explain to readers how they should behave during the war. Certainly there is ample evidence in the home-front literature that patriotic Northerners were expected to praise heroic soldiers, sacrificing wives, and tireless nurses. But there is also a large amount of publication suggesting that such patriotic sacrifice was a personal *decision* and not an obligation of citizenship. All sorts of evidence from the home front suggests that earnest, pro-war civilians had substantial freedom to decide how they wished to behave, free from the fear that they would fall outside the bounds of public approval. Four very different examples will have to suffice to illustrate this larger point.

In November 1861, *Arthur's Home Magazine*—a popular monthly—tackled the issue head on in an essay on "Our Duty." Timothy Shay Arthur began by arguing that no true patriot "can, in this crisis, stand aloof from the conflict." Such language seemed to suggest that he was going to inspire his readers to grand deeds, but as the essay unfolded Arthur's fundamental point was not that ordinary citizens should undertake great sacrifices or personal risks, but that all who care for the cause must "speak out boldly for the right" rather than sitting passively. Moreover, true patriots should "trust the government" and "not grow impatient" in the months to come. This advice would be echoed by quite a few authors in the years to come, perhaps most famously in Charles Stillé's popular pamphlet, *How a Free People Conduct a Long War.* Time and again these exhortatory texts ended up agreeing that the duty of the true patriot was to support the war and the government, and not grow restive about slow progress. That is, the sacrifice they expected was in declining to complain even when they were disappointed with military events or political decisions.

In the fall of 1862, the North turned to a state militia draft to fill the ranks (to be followed the next year by federal conscription legislation). On the face of it, conscription would seem to be the ultimate statement that all should be prepared to sacrifice equally for the cause. And much of the home front satire was directed at those men who went to ridiculous lengths to dodge the draft. But upon further inspection, most of this public commentary about conscription, and about those who were trying to avoid it, actually defined the issue in different terms. Consider the editorial stance offered by the strongly prowar *Chicago Tribune*. From early in the war, the *Tribune* had called for a draft, making the persistent argument that such a policy would properly distribute the burdens of war to all citizens. When the draft finally became law, the paper seemed thrilled, declaring that now "the traitor stands exposed, or he takes his place in the ranks to do citizen's duty." But despite all this bellicose language, the *Tribune* was remarkably sympathetic towards those men who had no inclination to carry a gun and who presented some legitimate excuse, opting instead to pay a three hundred dollar commutation fee. "If a man is adverse to serving from any cause, whether from a dread of the fatigues of the service, from the inconvenience of leaving his business, or from hostility, or aversion to the war, he can at any rate save himself from the hardship, or inconvenience, or the wickedness, if he so regards it, of participating in the war, by the payment of three hundred dollars." (August 25, 1862)

The wartime press reveals many comparable statements from other papers. How do we reconcile this forgiving attitude towards men who preferred not to serve, with the scathing mockery of those who dodged the draft? The answer is deceptively simple. The cultural consensus was that good citizens follow the rules. That is, a good citizen happily gave his name to the draft enroller and patiently waited to see if his name was called. At that point, the conscript was required by law to either present himself for military service or, if he chose, pay the commutation fee, hire a substitute, or demonstrate that he was legally exempt because of a medical infirmity or some other approved reason. So long as the drafted man had a good reason to prefer to remain at home (and the popular culture seemed surprisingly generous in making that assessment), and he followed the rules in doing so, he deserved no public scorn.

If published sources devoted considerable energy to evaluating the behavior of conscripts and potential enlistees, these sources had almost as much to say about how Northern women should behave during the war. When it came to supporting the war effort, a broad consensus agreed that patriotic women—mothers, wives, girlfriends—should not stand in the way if their menfolk wanted to enlist. (The interesting corollary here is that there seemed to be substantial feeling that men should yield to the objections of women.) But what of the broader obligations of patriotic women? Like the discussions of men, although the popular writings routinely praised selfless women who volunteered to support the cause, there seemed to be no notion that women on the home front had a duty to make voluntary sacrifices.

In another of the war's most famous pamphlets, an anonymous Northern woman penned *A Few Words in Behalf of the Loyal Women of the United States*. The essence of this fascinating 1863 pamphlet was that Southern women were earning more praise than Northern women because the Confederate cause had demanded great sacrifice of its citizens, whereas patriotic Northerners experience "moments when we feel ashamed, almost, of living comfortably; of reading fresh and pleasant books or enjoying social gatherings; of giving our children and young people the indulgences common to their age; of letting our thoughts wander to a happy future, unmindful of what sorrow and suffering may lie between us and that perhaps distant time." The author reassured her middle-class readers that they should feel proud of their patriotism even though the war was not necessarily forcing them to sacrifice. Similar themes appeared in home-front short stories in which timid characters—and, by extension, the readers—were reassured that the Union already had plenty of nurses and patriotic volunteers, and thus those individuals who preferred to stay at home should feel good about themselves so long as they supported the war effort in their words and thoughts. All could rest assured that they would surely step forward if their nation really needed them.

Throughout the war years, Northerners turned to Christian ministers for guidance about how they should respond to the crisis. A large number of these ministers chose to publish and distribute sermons on the war, often explaining that they did so at the urgings of their flocks. The result was a large number of published pamphlets on various aspects of Christian duty during wartime. Although these messages varied in their specifics, many themes recur over and over again. Dozens of pamphlets reassured readers that Christians had a moral duty to support just wars, and that the Union cause was indeed just. On at least two occasions, drafted ministers took to the pulpit to explain to their flocks why they were going off to serve the Union, rather than seeking an exemption. But here, again, the message was almost always framed around a call for patriotic Northerners to support the war effort with their thoughts and words, rather than any suggestion that they had a duty to make personal sacrifices to that cause.

In 1864, Boston's Reverend F. D. Huntington published his own thoughts on Christian duty in wartime. "Doubtless every citizen must do everything in his ability, according to the obvious rules and common-sense conditions of success, to render this impending movement physically powerful," he wrote.

> As a true patriot, and a true Christian,—and it cannot be too often repeated that he can never be a true Christian without being a true patriot,—he will uphold and help the forces that represent the faith that is in him and the cause he holds right and dear, by his gifts, by his daily speech, by his public spirit and attention to the public interest, by all cheerful, patient, prompt, untiring sacrifices.

Much like Anthony's patriotic essay on "duty" three years earlier, or the *Chicago Tribune* editorial of the following year, Rev. Huntington spoke eloquently of the need to support the war effort, but those expectations were balanced by a host of modifiers about "common sense" and each individual's personal ability. The reader was left with the message that patriots have a duty to be "cheerful" and "patient," but further sacrifice was largely left to the individual's assessment of his or her own abilities and inclinations.

The Union war experience is a fascinating case study of a democratic nation engaged in a massive military conflict. Scholars have tended to focus on those Northerners who actively dissented, and the actions of the government in response to such efforts. This essay has shifted the focus to consider what Northern society expected of those civilians who claimed to support the war. The messages embedded in the nation's popular culture are a useful window into that society.

On the one hand, Northerners would not tolerate hypocrites, liars, and cheats, particularly when such people profited from their misdeeds. Moreover, folks who purported to favor the Union cause were expected to maintain their cheerful enthusiasm when the going got tough. On the other hand, while the popular culture surely celebrated those who sacrificed for the cause, the printed message—in fiction, poems, editorials, pamphlets and cartoons—almost never indicated that citizens had any "duty" to make personal sacrifices for the cause. The idea that the benefits of citizenship came along with obligations and duties that might require personal sacrifice is completely absent from this nineteenth-century public conversation.

Time and again over four years of war, the cultural message to Northern citizens seemed to be that the Civil War presented individuals with choices and options, not unbending duties and obligations. And the collective gamble was that enough Americans would choose to make enough sacrifices that the Union would triumph.

Panel II Discussion

Following the presentations in Panel II: Internal Dissent in the Confederacy and the Union, panelists Carol Sheriff, Stephanie McCurry, Stephen V. Ash, and J. Matthew Gallman further discussed the topics.

Carol Sheriff: I wanted to start by picking up on the point that Matt ended with. In the North, it was possible to not be entirely anti-war or entirely pro-war. There was an ambivalent middle ground. I wanted to ask if the rest of you could reflect on the way that did or did not play itself out in the Confederacy. Are they rebelling against the war, the Confederacy, the planter elite? How much should we interpret this as the war opening fissures that were already there in society and how much do we see it as being anti-war?

Stephanie McCurry: It goes back to my own philosophy of history, which is to look at non-elites—it has emerged as an axiom of my thinking that most important changes come out of necessity. People do not choose radical change in a world of options; they are pushed into situations that press them to the wall, and then they make choices that are radical and drive change in that moment. The women in the Confederacy that I am interested in are non-slaveholders, yeoman, and poor white women. These women do not choose their new relationship to the government. Nobody expects the Confederate government to take this activist role that it takes, but it has to. The Confederacy is a non-industrial country fighting an industrial power. It cannot even cast its own national seal or make its own guns—it has to build up the industrial capacity.

The Confederacy also has to tax people to support the war effort, and it has an agricultural population. It is sending out a swarm of agents—women describe them as being like a plague of locusts—that comes across the countryside and goes into these women's barns and takes food out of them. These women are writing their husbands in the army and saying, "Do they mean us? They are going to take ten percent of everything I grow while you are gone?" There is an incredible intimacy that they are forced into with the Confederate government, or even the state government, that they do not choose. Then they attempt to use whatever leverage they have to survive in this situation.

What is striking is that there are some women who are part of kinship networks or community networks that are openly Unionist. There are tons of anti-secessionists before the war, especially in the Upper South, and some of these communities never change their minds. After conscription, that is a criminalized position and not a matter of choice. There are people there who really are anti-Confederate and are organized in an anti-Confederate way, such as in east Tennessee. I would say the vast majority of women that I read about are dissenting because of survival. I find these women in North Carolina, in Georgia, and in Mississippi. There are these openly anti-Confederate pockets of dissent, and some of them are significant. Some of them are also, on rare occasions, anti-slavery. They do not talk about the cause and they do not talk in nationalist terms because they are not invested in the success of the Confederacy. They are just struggling to get through this incredibly chaotic and insupportable moment. Four years is not necessarily that long on the scale of wars of independence, but for rural people who cannot make enough food, whose food supply on the hoof is being destroyed every time the army comes near them—they are pushed to the wall and they mobilize and push back. This is not feminism; they are not choosing women's rights. This is what people do when they have to survive, and I do not think it has anything to do with the Confederate cause. I think it is damaging to the Confederate cause, but I do not think that is the intent.

Stephen V. Ash: I think that if we could send a television reporter back into the past with a microphone and stick it in the face of a poor white in the occupied South who had run to a Yankee garrison and asked them why they are rebelling, he or she would not have said that they were rebelling. They were responding to specific circumstances. They were, in many cases, responding to an opportunity, but their actions were driven by hardships in the countryside and a hope for a better life behind Union lines. To ask them why they were rebelling, however, is to assume a revolutionary consciousness at work there. I do not think that is true, except for a very small percentage that wanted to overthrow Southern society and make a new world, to bring down the aristocracy and bring themselves up. I do not think most of them, though, saw their experience in that way, or had that intention. It is historians that look at a moment and call it a revolutionary momentum. It might have had that effect, but the intentionality was not there.

Carol Sheriff: Was the pull to Union lines a pragmatic pull or an ideological one?

Stephen V. Ash: It was a pragmatic pull in the sense that they knew that they could find shelter there, that there were camps set up, and that there were Northern missionaries who came down to teach the poor whites just as they did the slaves. There were opportunities there, such as the possibility of jobs. It was a matter of seeking opportunity, then, and not a matter of making revolution.

J. Matthew Gallman: During the Civil War, the Confederate government is a much more oppressive government than the one in the North. It is much more involved in the lives of civilians. Everything that the North is trying to accomplish during the war is done through market forces, not through explicitly taking items from people. This creates a really interesting irony: The Confederacy becomes the country fighting a total war.

Stephanie McCurry: A political scientist said something really stunning. He measured the sizes of the Union and Confederate governments, coming from the same base. What he says is that the

Leviathan government is the Confederate government and that the United States did not have a government that big until the New Deal. It is really stunning. You talk about revolutionary; that is revolutionary. They wrote the sovereignty of the states into the Confederate Constitution, and the ink was not even dry before the necessities of the Confederacy forced them into building this top-down, centralized country. It is one of the most interesting things that happens and I think it propels a lot of response on the part of ordinary people. The government is supposed to be building a new country, and there are some very grand ideas about becoming a big player on the stage of nations. From the beginning, though, over ninety percent of the national budget is the budget of the War Department. From the get-go, the Confederate States of America is essentially the War Department.

J. Matthew Gallman: Since we are in Virginia, I feel compelled to mention Robert E. Lee. One of the great myths about Robert E. Lee is that he remained loyal to Virginia as opposed to the Confederacy. Robert E. Lee's loyalty to Virginia vis-á-vis either federal government lasts for about a week and a half, maybe two weeks. In fact, he is a major Confederate nationalist during the Civil War, much more so than he is loyal to Virginia.

Carol Sheriff: Matt, were there any manifestations of dissent along the lines that we see here in the Confederacy in the Union as well?

J. Matthew Gallman: You do not so much have economic dissent against the government, but what you do have are labor unions that form and strike. There are moments where the federal government goes after unions, especially in the coal fields. You have resistance efforts to the draft, most famously in New York. Actually, during the New York City Draft Riot, around ten percent of the people arrested are women. The women who are arrested are mostly older women, and the best argument would be that they are rioting because their sons are drafted. That is a supposition, but I think a fair one. To answer your question, there is economic dissent, and political dissent on different tiers. The political dissent goes from the judicial dissent about the nature of the National Banking Act to questions about conscription.

Stephanie McCurry: I just want to say something funny: Some of those women rioting in the New York City Draft Riots are rioting because they are Irish and that is how they have learned to settle disputes. [Audience laughter] There is a serious point there, though. We always talk about war with the assumption that women are not centrally engaged or do not usually resort to acts of violence. That is a fiction, and it depends on your political culture. Women crack heads and go into the streets to take up armed struggle in all kinds of ways. If you read the transcriptions of the draft riots, it is clear that there is an immigrant population there with a different political history, and that is part of the reason that they are acting in the way that they do. That gets written out because now they are New Yorkers, but really they are Irish immigrants.

Stephen V. Ash: If I did not make it clear in my presentation, a lot of these poor whites in the occupied South who are taking action are women. When the mountain people descended on Beersheba Springs, my sense is that most of them were, in fact, women who were raiding those cabins and the hotel.

Carol Sheriff: When we talk about the draft riots, we talk about the confluence of the draft, big government, and emancipation. I had hoped that we could talk a little bit about the influence of emancipation on the white populations of both the Union and the Confederacy. I want to focus on the poorer folks in particular, but we can speak more generally as well.

Stephen V. Ash: Emancipation was one of those things I mentioned at the end of my talk that drove a wedge between the blacks and the poor whites, and, in a sense, drove the poor whites and the aristocrats together. This is one of the things that put the brakes on the revolutionary momentum. I came across a number of instances where poor white men went out of their way to recapture runaway slaves and return them to their masters, from whom they received a commendation. Had there been no emancipation in the occupied South, I think there might have been more revolutionary momentum. It was a countervailing pressure.

Stephanie McCurry: What is striking to me is how little interaction there was between the planter class and the struggling mass of non-slaveholding people in the same communities. There is a geographical element to this. The very wealthy slaveholding communities are always located along the rivers, in the rich lowlands. The non-slaveholding communities are spread across different parts of the state, or even different parts of the same county or parish. On the whole, I agree with what Steve said about this. There are only very rare occasions where I see poor white women expressing any concern about slaves and a human concern about their wellbeing and the necessity of emancipation. It happens, but it is extremely rare.

At the same time, the hostility between planters and what is left behind of the yeomanry around the question of slavery is enormous. A lot of it has to do with the way that the planters were able to, as the yeoman saw it, cause this war and then protect themselves from the costs of waging it. In a sense, it is not that they are making an alliance with slaves or that they are concerned about slaves, because they are not. However, they grow increasingly and more directly hostile to slavery and slaveholding because of the ways it has distorted the practices of their own community and the social policies of the government.

The most direct conflicts that I see are the conflicts that come between slaveholding men and non-slaveholding men. The slaveholders encourage local men to join up early and go to war. They fund and arm these military units and get themselves elected officers. When they do this, they make very grandiose promises to the communities in big speeches or flag presentation ceremonies. They promise to take care of the women and children, and at that moment they probably mean it. Some of these yeomen go to war, signing up for three months and then say, "It is planting time, I need to go home." Or, they get sent out of state and complain about it because they are worried about their families. Then, the planters and the leaders within the community, who encouraged them to go, are nowhere to be found. The women are writing the governors and the Secretary of War and they are denouncing these people right and left. They say, "Put him in the army, he ain't no use to us at home." By 1863, the only way to stay out of the army is if you have a civil service job that is in a protected category, including the commissioners of the poor. The women denounce these men roundly to the governor, and if you are in the right state, the governor listens. The hostility between slaveholders and non-slaveholders has increased exponentially, I would say because of the way slaveholders handle their part of the responsibility for waging the war.

Carol Sheriff: Were there any places in the Confederate South that are relatively untouched by the war?

Stephen V. Ash: If you mean untouched by the Union invasion and occupation, then yes. Large areas of the South, in fact. If you look at it geographically, only a small portion of the South was actually invaded by Union armies. I would be surprised if more than ten percent of the entire geographical extent of the Confederacy was actually invaded and held by the Union army during the war. Large stretches go completely untouched, Texas being an example.

Carol Sheriff: How do you think that would compare to places in the Union where large extents are not touched by the military?

J. Matthew Gallman: If you think of the Union as including border territory that gets captured, like Tennessee, much of the Union never gets touched by invasion. The Confederate army was in Gettysburg for about seventy-two hours, but the battle left behind masses of dead horses, which had a huge impact on the community for months. That being said, it is nothing akin to what is going on in Virginia or South Carolina. We tend to think of the entire Confederacy as being under invasion. Someone did a study a couple of years ago of how many local courthouses were destroyed by the war, and it was about ten percent.

Stephanie McCurry: I think that we can very easily underestimate this. There are two things going on here: One is that 3.5 million slaves end up inside Confederate territory and they have to fight their fight against slavery and their masters exactly where they lived, which is dangerous. Thavolia gave some incredible examples of this, and it is happening all over the place. I think the narrative of the black soldier has really distracted us from this process. It is as if every slave man made it to the Union army and enlisted and fought. Most of them are trying to work inside Confederate lines to do what they can to push against Confederate success. That is a battlefront between slaveholders and slaves, and it is inside Confederate lines.

The other thing that we have to remember is that the army controls the food supply by 1863, which means nobody is outside war. The Union army might not be there, but the Confederate agents are there and they are taking food out of your barn, they are taking your sons into the army, and they are leaving you at home with infant children and a farm to till. In that sense, there is no place that is untouched by war. Eighty-five percent of men aged fifteen to sixty-five go off to war. I do not think that we can really grasp what that means. Therefore, it is not where the army is and it certainly is not just about where the Union army is. It is about the damage the Confederate army and Confederate mobilization do. There are many places where women left behind on the home front are dealing with Confederate cavalry, home guards, and militia units that are engaged in the wildest depredations on the community itself. The women write letters to the government and say, "Who needs the Union army? These people are destroying us." There is no "outside" in the Confederacy. There are places that people run to, where whites try to "refugee" to, especially in Texas or Mississippi. However, even if you read the correspondence from the governor's office in Mississippi, it is a moving target. It starts out with dateline: Jackson. Next time it is dateline: Meridian. They are moving south on the run, and this is after 1862.

Parts of South Carolina right off the coast were invaded in November 1861, but twenty or thirty miles inland does not fall until Christmas 1864. That is three full years of trying to keep your slaves in check and trying to keep the white population in check, just twenty miles up the river from where the navy is posted at Hilton Head. Ed Ayers said this morning that there are "micro-geographies" of war, and I think that is a really important concept. With the Confederacy, I think because it is so unprepared to wage war on this scale, the efforts that they have to make and the burdens that they put on their own population are beyond anything that we can imagine.

Carol Sheriff: I was wondering if all of you could reflect on how these "passive dissenters" helped to shape the post-war history.

Stephen V. Ash: I have always found it interesting that the Union military victory in the Civil War decided a couple of questions very definitely. By April or May 1865, the Union military had made sure that the South was going to be brought back into the Union, that secession was dead, and that the slaves were free. That also leaves a whole lot of questions unanswered. Among those questions is what the shape of the post-war South is going to be. A lot of the answer to that question has its origin in what happened on the Confederate home front from 1861-1865. It became clear that slaves were going to press for a broader kind of freedom. It became clear that many poor whites were anxious to improve their status. I think what we see in the Reconstruction era is a natural outgrowth of many of these conflicts that arise in the Confederacy and it is going to shape what the post-war South looks like.

Carol Sheriff: One of the things that Eric Foner has written about is how, in some ways, the failures of Reconstruction were due to Northern citizens losing interest in it by the early 1870s. Do we see early signs of a lack of interest during the war itself?

J. Matthew Gallman: Northerners are okay with paying for a war, which is mostly paid for with bonds, not taxes. They are less okay with continuing to spend money on the South after the war and they are less okay with an experiment that many people, including many people on the left, feel is not working. Another big legacy is that for the four years of the war, most of the organized women's movement in the North, both suffrage and otherwise, agreed to set aside that kind of agitation in favor of abolition and winning the war. As soon as the war is over, the powers that be essentially declare that it's the black man's hour and give the vote to African-American men. This makes white women in the North who are engaged in the political reform movement very unhappy with what has happened. There is also a big question on how our Constitution is written. The Fourteenth Amendment is written and then almost immediately unwritten in lots of important ways, such as the nature of citizenship.

Stephanie McCurry: There is a moment where the women that I have been interested in emerge publicly as a force and the government has to answer to them. However, this does not continue after the war. I think that we have not done the right kind of research or asked the right kinds of questions. I also think that, on the whole, we do not know enough about the yeomanry and what happens to them as a social class after the war. We know that in the long run a lot of these people lose their land and these communities change, but we do not really know how quickly it happens. As is often the case, the fate of the women is tied up with the fate of the families in the community. I do think that they remain consequential in certain kinds of state policies, such as support of widows and orphans that these very broke state governments are trying to do after the war is over.

The only thing that I am really sure about without the kind of research we would need is that there is no going back. There is no continuity here. Something fundamental has changed. Slavery was the foundation of Southern society from the end of the seventeenth century through to the 1860s, and when you take it away you have got to remake that world. It takes a lot of work: social, cultural, ideological, and political. Women's place is remade within there too. I think it is remade in internal psyches, between mistresses and their house servants. The transformation happens at every level: from the marriage and the family, to the employer/employee relationship, to the highest levels of government. It is amazing how little we actually know about non-elite whites in all of this. Much of the attention on women after the war is on women's role in Confederate memorialization, which is a cultural lead that women take in remembering and honoring Confederate dead. Honestly, though, I ask whether we know if women from non-slaveholding families joined these associations or did they just go back to the desperate activity of survival? We still do not know fundamental things like that. We know a little bit, and we make that the whole story, but there is so much else that we need to know.

J. Matthew Gallman: Can you speak to the role of demographics on post-war Southern women when there is this whole age cohort of men that has been totally decimated?

Stephanie McCurry: Demographers are really frustrating on this point because they claim that even with this number of Confederate dead, it does not actually affect the reproduction of the population or marriage patterns. I find it incomprehensible that you can lose seven hundred twenty thousand men and not have a demographic impact. I think it is something that we think we see—lots of widows, the idea of widows remarrying very young men or very old men—but they claim it does not actually have a demographic effect.

Stephen V. Ash: Part of the reason we have a hard time answering that question is that we do not know which "South" we are talking about. If you are talking about Confederate memorial associations in the post-Civil War South, the women were mostly elite. Keep in mind, though, that they were mostly urban women too. That was an elite, urban phenomenon. What about the vast mass of women who were out in the countryside? They were not forming memorial associations.

Stephanie McCurry: They must have been honoring the Confederate dead, though, building cemeteries and tending the graves. I imagine that that must have been happening, but building it up and linking it to a Lost Cause politics? That is a whole different position. I think there are some things that we actually need to research before we conclude.

Panel III: Question and Answer

Following the Panel II: Internal Dissent in the Confederacy and the Union discussion, all panelists gathered to answer audience-submitted questions.

Scott Reynolds Nelson: We have a whole bunch of questions from the audience, organized by student volunteers. I'm just going to start right in.

Audience question: Given the immense body of scholarship on the topic of the Civil War, what areas of study do you think have been under-examined?

Stephen Kantrowitz: I think the West is as yet under-examined. That's changing very rapidly, and we will see books in the next few years that will really change that. In many ways the fate of slavery in the West is as central of a dynamic to the coming war as there is. When the war comes, the West—at least the non-Confederate West—becomes a footnote to the struggle, until the war ends, and then it immediately comes back as the territory to be seized from Native Americans and transformed into part of the American domain. That's a very odd elision, and the task immediately confronting us, I would say, is to find a way to fully integrate the North-South struggle and the East-West struggle, both of which are central to mid-nineteenth-century American history.

Stephanie McCurry: The way to do it is to say that it's a struggle over the extent of the federal government and sovereignty. They're both a struggle over states' rights or Native American sovereignty;

they're part of the same struggle but they're always organized sequentially: first the Civil War and then the war against the Indians in the West.

The other thing that I would say is really understudied is exactly what Thavolia is writing about: refugees. The federal government creates an agency in the middle of the Civil War, the Bureau of Refugees, Freedmen, and Abandoned Lands, and we forgot the word refugee until she reminded us. We had gotten it lost in terms of slaves and contraband and all these kinds of things. It's really amazing what she does when she reminds us that these people are refugees, because then you start to think about how central the refugee crisis is in other wars. People who write about World War II are much better about writing about this than we are. The Civil War is a humanitarian crisis, as Thavolia says, and that brings it back into focus. We have not really written enough about that. The consequences in the postwar period, with all due deference to Eric and his absolutely magisterial book on Reconstruction, we have that whole period organized. He organized it so we can think through it and teach it, but what is lost in the order is the chaos of people who stagger home from war to devastated communities, who are dislocated by war, impoverished by war, two-thirds of the capital wiped out, no functioning government. What is the human experience of that, trying to rebuild a world? It would be interesting to look at something really close in, one or two years after the war, and see: What is the human experience of that, of trying to put the world back together at the end?

Stephen V. Ash: I'd like to see more about the transition from war to peace. We tend to think in a dichotomous way about the Civil War: it ended in the spring of 1865 and then Reconstruction began. But actually there's a transition there, from the spring, through the summer and the fall and beyond, in which it was a process of ending a war and beginning a reconstruction. Only a few historians, including Leon Litwack in his book on the black experience, have seen that as a process, a seamless process, from war to peace.

Scott Reynolds Nelson: Greg Downs has been working on the financial side of the Civil War; one of the things that's hard to understand is that once the United States goes back to the gold standard, it's very difficult to sell US bonds anymore because the safe haven is no longer in US bonds. That inability to sell bonds is part of the reason the army has to shrink so drastically the way that it does in April of 1865, which is part of the reason why Reconstruction is as unsettled and violent as it is in 1866 through 1868. So there's a financial story that underlies a situation that we don't fully understand, in a way connecting the early history of Reconstruction to the latter part.

In one of the chapters of our *People at War* book, Carol and I talk about occupation. Reconstruction policy starts in 1862. The Union is talking about what Reconstruction is going to look like in 1862 and this is partly why we asked Steve to join us; he's one of the few people who really does talk about the occupation as a kind of Reconstruction policy. Lincoln does some peculiar and interesting things during the war, besides the Lieber Code, and one of them is creating provisional governors. He says that Tennessee is just Memphis, and that Virginia is just Alexandria, and then calls these reconstructed states and builds the freed peoples' communities that rotate around them, calling on labor. This is an attempt to reconstruct during the war itself, and so it would be interesting to look at the long history of Reconstruction, actually starting in the middle of the war.

J. Matthew Gallman: One thing that strikes me is that there is a huge population, North and South, of individuals who become soldiers. There is a little bit of scholarship on the African American soldier and that transition, but if you think about it, in 1860, very few Americans have much relationship with the federal government or even with government at all. Soldiers are really in a very different kind of cultural place in terms of all sorts of things, like how you get things, how you're provided for things, how rules are done, what the structure of order is—all these things. Soldier culture is an interesting thing, and I've seen no one who has examined what happens to these ex-soldiers. We have good scholarship on veterans but not on the cultural experience of having been a soldier and how that translates into your postwar life. For instance, in 1877 there are fascinating labor riots. If you look at the behavior of militia groups made up of Union veterans and militia groups that are not made of Union veterans, the behavior is dramatically different. This is a legacy of having been soldiers, even though they're no longer in the federal military.

Thavolia Glymph: There is a great deal of new work on what happens with demobilization and we find soldiers—those who have fought on either side of the Civil War—are fighting in the West; we find them in the native wars; we find them later in the Philippines and in Cuba. In a new project, I'm looking at men who joined the Egyptian army in 1869 and served there for almost ten years. They were ex-Confederate and Union officers, which brings me to the point, which is that among the topics we really need to study is the West, and not just the native question but also the race question. I am intrigued by the new work that embraces the whole question of coolie labor, the question of Asian Americans in San Francisco, of Asian populations who moved in large numbers to the Pacific Northwest, to Oregon and Washington, about the migration of people from Asia, from Hawaii and all the kinds of labor questions that arose in the postwar era that were very much connected to questions of race and race management in the wartime era. David Roediger and Elizaebth Esch have done some important work on this in their new book, *The Production of Difference: Race and the Management of Labor in U.S. History*. There are lots of areas that we need to study.

Stephen Kantrowitz: There's a book out by Stacey Smith, *Freedom's Frontier: California and the Struggle over Unfree Labor, Emancipation, and Reconstruction*, which is a study of all of the variety of unfree and semi-free labor systems that existed in California in the mid-nineteenth century, before, during, and after the Civil War.

Thavolia Glymph: The new book by Kornel Chang, *Pacific Connections: The Making of the U.S.-Canadian Borderlands*, does something similar.

Scott Reynolds Nelson: Audience question: Is there a document from your research that speaks to the lived human experience during this conflict? Is there a document that you can describe that gives you goosebumps or makes you think?

Stephanie McCurry: I have one. It's from a woman called Margaret Smith in North Carolina. In 1863 she wrote the governor a letter that describes in the most poignant terms imaginable the destruction of the yeomanry. You have to read the words aloud, because they're written phonetically; for example, "women" is spelled "wimmin." She said, "There was a time when we could call our husbands and our little children to our table, and have a plenty, and now we have become beggars and starvers and no way to help ourselves." It's a pretty succinct description of this proud independent yeoman class of people who could make what they needed on their own farms and didn't need to ask anybody for anything. The husbands are gone; the grown sons are gone; now she is trying to make a living out of that land with tiny little children. She is turning to the government, and the government is not there for her either.

Stephen V. Ash: I have recently been using a remarkable source. Within a year after the Civil War there was a major race riot in Memphis. A congressional investigating committee came to the city along with two other federal institutions. They started taking verbatim testimony from people who rarely get into the historical record: poor black people who had just come in from the countryside, who had lived all their lives as slaves. They were questioned very closely and the testimony in these records is voluminous. You learn not only how they lived in the black parts of town, where no newspaper reporter ever went; you learn how they spoke, the words and language they used. It's the kind of source on people of the mid-nineteenth century that's hard to find.

Eric Foner: I would like to add that finding documents from ordinary people whose voices you don't often hear is important and remarkable, but it's also important to read with real care the documents you thought you already knew. Let's take the Emancipation Proclamation, a pretty well-known document that everybody can read any time they want. When I was working on the Lincoln book, I actually saw things I had never seen before, partly because Lincoln is such a careful writer. Every single word is carefully chosen.

At one point in the Proclamation he actually addresses slaves directly. He says, "I urge you to go to work for reasonable wages." When I read that, I thought it was interesting that he put the word "reasonable" in there. He didn't just say go to work for wages, or just go to work. Go to work for reasonable wages. You have a right to decide whether the wages offered to you are reasonable or not. If they're not, you should demand reasonable wages. Why did he put that in? I don't know.

Later in that same document he addresses slaves again, saying "I urge you to refrain from violence." There was so much propaganda that if you decreed emancipation there would be a bloody uprising in the South and slaves would massacre their owners, and so on. "Refrain from violence," he says, but he doesn't stop there, "except in necessary self-defense." Now, why did he put in that they have a right to self-defense to protect the freedom that had just been decreed? He doesn't say just be peaceful; he says you have a right to defend this freedom that has just been acquired. I had never really thought about that before. Reading things carefully is very important for historians, even when the documents are very public and well known.

J. Matthew Gallman: I spent a lot of my life writing about Philadelphia during the Civil War and the home front. There is a marvelous diary by a woman named Emily Davis, which wasn't available at that time to access, though it is now online, through the Philadelphia Historical Society. Emily Davis was an African-American working woman living in Philadelphia who kept a diary. It's a wonderful source. I would have loved to read it online back in 1985 when I was writing my dissertation.

Stephen Kantrowitz: The sources that inspire me are the letterbooks of the paid agent of the government of Haiti, an abolitionist named James Redpath, whose job it was to recruit free black Americans to move to Haiti between 1859 and 1862. They were actively and in some cases successfully recruiting free blacks through 1862. Until the Emancipation Proclamation, it was not clear to everybody that the United States would be a reasonable home for the future. The Dred Scott decision had been passed; many states had moved toward re-enslavement or drastically limiting the rights of free black people; and the secession crisis brought movements toward deportation and all kinds of other restrictions. In 1861 Frederick Douglass was preparing to sail to Haiti to check it out, and it was the firing at Fort Sumter that dissuaded him from it. What that document does is remind me of how tenuous the claim to American citizenship was among African Americans, even as late as the first years of the war.

Thavolia Glymph: There are many documents that have made me stop in my tracks. Two come to mind: one is called "A Father's Prayer," a document that I found in an 1863 newspaper. This father said, "Our children are dying in the camps as we tote them from place to place." That was it. I remember transcribing it, typing it, in language that is, as Stephanie described, grammatically incorrect, phonetic spelling. I printed it and put it above my desk, and it keeps me going.

Another is a letter written in 1862 by Secretary of the Treasury Salmon P. Chase to another Northern man who was in the South. Chase wrote: "The black woman who works for me has two daughters, both of whom were stolen from her. Here is the information she has." She had given Chase descriptions of her daughters and their names and what she knew of the men who had purchased them in Louisiana.

It's a powerful document. The Secretary had taken the time to listen to this black woman who was his maid, and to write to somebody in Louisiana and ask him to help her. The guy eventually wrote back and said, "No, I can't help you because it's too disorganized here, and we can't track the daughters down." We talk about how emancipation comes, and sometimes we forget that some people were free while their family members were not yet free. People were still trying to find family members long after the war ended.

Scott Reynolds Nelson: I was working on a book about male friendships in Civil War prison camps, and had read probably thirty or forty Andersonville diaries. They were repetitious; and I tried to make sense of them, then Port Lookout diaries. Then I went to Andersonville and walked around the place, and as I was getting a sense of the space, it just kind of hit me, all of the descriptions and how they all fit together. I experienced the documents very differently, walking through there, and I started to cry. It was really very moving. There's a way in which visiting the ground really makes a difference. It's 150 years since, but there's a sense in which they speak to you. They can tell you something about a place that just makes those documents give you goosebumps.

Audience question: Some people, including historians, use the terms Southerners and Confederates interchangeably. As the work of the panelists clearly show, not all people who lived in the South supported the Confederacy. Do we need to redefine the basic terminology of the Civil War South?

Stephanie McCurry: I think there's an even deeper problem, although it's alleviating, which is that when we say "Southerners," we mean white Southerners. If you care about elegance in writing, you don't always want to have to qualify everything you say: white male Southerners; white women Southerners; enslaved Southerners. You have to decide how much you can tolerate of generalization and when it is important to be specific. There's no doubt: "Southerners" doesn't mean "white Southerners." This makes a big difference when you go out to talk about the Confederacy with African-American people in the audience, who are themselves Southerners, particularly older people who have lived with this particular history of the Confederacy all through their lives and are very relieved to hear a different story. I think it's really ingrained, to think of Southerners as white Southerners, although I think it's changing. Confederates and Southerners are just not the same thing.

In writing my book, I didn't expect to be so interested in secession. Secession was really hard to pull off. There were so many people opposed to it, not just in Virginia, but even in the Deep South. And then there's this war; we thought it had a unifying effect, but it didn't. Confederates and Southerners are not the same thing.

Stephen Kantrowitz: The circumstances of free black life make it very hard to tell who is a Southerner and who is not. Hiram Revels is born free black in North Carolina, educated in Ohio, travels to Mississippi with the Union army, becomes state senator in Mississippi, becomes the first black member of Congress, filling the seat left vacant by Jefferson Davis. Is he a Northerner, a Southerner, a carpetbagger? Yes, to all of these questions. The regional distinctions are less helpful than they might seem to be.

Scott Reynolds Nelson: There are colorful nouns, some of which are likely to cause offense, to describe white Southerners. We use yeoman because yeoman doesn't have that negative connotation. There are other terms in the documents that we look at that were used at the time that obviously we can't use.

Audience question: Given the lack of diversity in this audience, is the Civil War too painful a topic for African Americans or too far removed a topic for youth?

Thavolia Glymph: I don't think the Civil War is too painful a topic for African Americans; I think rather the way it has been presented has made it painful. For too long it has been presented as a story of white people, as a story of white Americans who fought a horrible war and then came back together when it was over and rejoined hands.

I grew up hearing about the Civil War and not being embarrassed by it, but I understand that in recent years some black people have been embarrassed by it, but it is only because of the way the story is told. The work of the scholars here and many others has demonstrated that black people played such a central role in this war, whether you talk about it from the Confederate side or the Union side or the American West. So the makeup of today's audience and similar audiences says something not about what black people did but about how we have told the story, which has resulted in their not being very interested. If you make the traditional battlefield the central story, and make generals and commanders and soldiers the central story without the women, the yeoman, or poor white women, or free black people, then it's a problem.

Scott Reynolds Nelson: Audience question: We've been discussing working class unrest during the Civil War. Does this dissent carry over into the postwar period, perhaps labor movements and others? How is it expressed?

Eric Foner: One question is how we define labor conflict. We tend to think in twentieth-century terms of factories and labor unions. There was an enormous amount of conflict in the South, on plantations and on farms after the war, among both poorer whites and former slaves trying to carve out new economic situations for themselves. Certainly in the North, the period after the Civil War was one of tremendous volatility, violent strikes, mine worker strikes, railroad worker strikes, and a very rapid rise of union membership in the late 1860s and 1870s. The labor conflict of the Civil War does flow over into the postwar period and there is a sense, both North and South, that the ordinary people have suffered the most. They say it's a rich man's war and a poor man's fight. Inflation in both societies was devastating for poorer people because in both societies there was so much paper money and prices rose enormously. That's another thing we could study more: trace out how the class conflict that emerges in the Civil War is played out in the Gilded Age, which lasts many years after the end of the Civil War.

Scott Reynolds Nelson: There were huge rice strikes in the South Carolina low country in the 1870s.

Eric Foner: That's labor conflict, though we tend to compartmentalize. That's a race issue, even though it's laborers on strike, whereas in the North it's a labor issue. We need to put those things together, so to speak.

Scott Reynolds Nelson: Eric, I've always wondered about the connection between the Northern union movement during the Civil War and the Democratic Party. The labor movement had a more Republican character by the 1880s and 1890s, but were the union workers and the Democratic Party linked in some way?

Eric Foner: It really depends where we're talking about. In the cities of the North, yes. Certainly in New York City and big cities. But in smaller communities—and remember, most industry was outside of big cities at the time—places like Lowell, Massachusetts, or Troy, New York, it wasn't really associated with either party, necessarily. In the Gilded Age, there was a lot of independent labor politics, the Greenback labor party, a lot of local labor politics. Today we have more of a two-party system, but back in the nineteenth century there were all sorts of parties around. The Republican Party was just ten years old when it came to power and in the later nineteenth century, there were populists, the Greenbackers, local parties, the Readjusters here in Virginia, and others. So the political system was much more fluid back then. There was a lot more openness to third parties and local parties than we seem to have nowadays.

Scott Reynolds Nelson: Audience question: Back to the West and the war—How were Native Americans in the South affected by the war?

Stephen Kantrowitz: Most native people and all native nations had been removed from the South by the time of the Civil War, but that doesn't mean that the experience of southern tribes wasn't at issue, because in Indian territory where the Cherokee, Choctaw, Creek, Chickasaw, and Seminole had been removed earlier in the nineteenth century, factional politics in many ways followed slaveholding. Some factions of the elites in these tribes were slaveholding and some were not, and that pretty much determined whether they were willing to treat with the Confederacy or not. Then there were civil wars within the tribes that ended up drawing Confederate and Union armies into Indian territory and a war raged between Kansas and Indian territory, what is now Oklahoma, for most of the Civil War. That was part of the western theater of the war, and it drew in generals on the Confederate side and units on the Union side. It's a fairly dramatic story, and it continued on after Appomattox.

Eric Foner: This is one of those areas that cry out for more study. There is work being done about Native Americans and the Civil War, not so much in fighting, but how the war affects Native Americans. The Civil War was a disaster for Native Americans, North, South, and West. There were Indian massacres all over the place. One irony: in order to defend the Union in the East, during the secession crisis, even while he was defending Fort Sumter, Lincoln pulled troops out of forts in the West. Native Americans were bitterly opposed to this because, whatever their problems with the soldiers, soldiers were often protecting them from violence by the settlers. That unleashed a lot of conflict, even as the Civil War was beginning.

Here's a little factoid: Those tribes that sided with the Confederacy, and therefore were on the losing side, were the only slave-owners who were required by the Union to give land to their emancipated slaves. The famous forty acres and a mule never happened in the South, but the Cherokee, the Creek tribes had not only to free the slaves, but also absorb them into the tribe and give them land. They were the only emancipated slaves who got their acreage.

The Civil War is still with us, in that the status of those slaves of Native Americans is still being adjudicated today. Just recently the Cherokee Nation tried to expel from the nation the descendants of black Cherokee slaves, who have been Cherokee for 150 years. It is mostly because of casino money, frankly. It's now in federal court, and the question is, can a federal court tell a tribe who is a member of that tribe? There are all sorts of complicated legal issues involved. That's a Civil War question. It comes right out of the Civil War and it's still in our courts 150 years later.

J. Matthew Gallman: A small irony connected to that is that the

United States conducted foreign policy at the point of a bayonet even during the Civil War. Some Union volunteers from California ended up quite famously fighting in the East, including one regiment that gets connected to Philadelphia. A large portion of the Californians who joined the Union army during the Civil War actually were sent just barely east to fight Native Americans in ways that had nothing to do with the Civil War. They were just engaged in federal foreign policy against Indians.

Thavolia Glymph: Federal policy had a lot to do with the formation of this new nation state, as Stephanie mentioned earlier, and one of the most devastating massacres of native peoples happened in 1864 at Sand Creek. Some Californians and Washingtonians and Oregonians moved east to fight on the prairies. Native people had long-standing wars with Mexico over the border. That war becomes transformed during the Civil War as US troops move into those territories, and Confederates are trying to refugee their slaves into Texas and it all becomes one massive war that we have mistakenly divided into North-South, East-West. It's one massive national war about the state, about who belongs to the state and who can be denied. It goes back to Eric's point about the Cherokee continuing to this day to question the legitimacy of people of African descent whose history as Cherokees dates back to before the removal of the Cherokee in the 1820s and 1830s.

Stephanie McCurry: One thing that I would add that is connected to all of these points is that because the Confederacy was thrown so quickly on the defensive and shrunk within its originally quite huge boundaries, it's easy to forget the ambitions that the Confederacy had at the outset. If you read Alexander Stephens's speech, he appeals to the border states and especially to Virginia to turn away from the Union. Basically they say that the Southwest belongs to them; Cuba belongs to them; maybe Brazil will join them. The question that Steve raised before about the West does not go away.

In fact, that is one of the main reasons for the war, especially on the part of Texans. Secession for Texans means that they own the West. We're being cut off from it, and who are you to tell us it doesn't belong to us? We have already gotten a third of Mexico ten years ago and we are intending to get a lot more of Mexico: Chihuahua, Sonora. They really want to move south and west, and there is this brief moment when they do. They move into New Mexico and Arizona and they meet the Union army there.

Historians like Brian DeLay at Berkeley are doing a kind of Native American history that wasn't being done ten years ago. They have reminded us that huge chunks of the American West are dominated by certain kinds of tribes like the Comanche or the Apache, which is the reason why the Confederacy is not really beat in the Southwest so much by the Union as it is by the Native Americans. Spain couldn't control the northern border of Mexico; Mexico couldn't when they took it; the United States couldn't when they took it, and they couldn't in the 40s, 50s, or 60s. So it's really a war against both these armies and Native American people. The Union army doesn't have the upper hand; the Confederate army doesn't have the upper hand, but there's this imperialist push west. For about twelve months it works, and we forget because we're focused on the East, but that was their ambition. It's interesting to ask that counter-factual: What if the Confederacy had hung on for longer? What if they had been more successful? How many parts would North America have broken into? We have this sense of manifest destiny, that it had to end up the way it did, but it didn't. It could have gone so many ways, and one of the reasons it didn't was that Native American people weren't completely disempowered. They still controlled big swaths of the Southwest.

Stephen Kantrowitz: One scholar named Walter Johnson has made the point that Stephanie is making about the slaveholders' imagination of the future, what he calls their "pro-slavery futurity." It's an important way of imagining what they thought was possible. They weren't thinking about being restricted to an eleven-state or even fifteen-state Confederacy but to a much larger Caribbean empire. That's also the reason Lincoln can't accept the Crittenden Resolutions, the territorial compromise of redrawing the 36-30 compromise line. As he famously says, this amounts to a perpetual declaration of war on all of the peoples and tribes from here to the

Tierra del Fuego.

Stephanie McCurry: Didn't he give in on Arizona at one point?

Eric Foner and Stephen Kantrowitz: (in unison) New Mexico.

Stephen Kantrowitz: The irony is that as soon as the Civil War is done, the US government declares war on all the peoples and tribes north of the republic of Mexico.

Scott Reynolds Nelson: You can see that in the "Cotton is King" speech by Hammond, that story of the Knights of the Golden Circle—the idea of the Caribbean as a kind of natural empire. He says that New Orleans is the capital, and that this is an empire that can be built entirely on cotton. The rest of the nation depends on the cotton that is produced in the South and that needs to end. After Andrew Jackson conquers Florida and blows up Negro Fort, he says, "For another ten thousand dollars, I'm ready to take Cuba."

Stephanie McCurry: I don't think they were wrong about Cuba. The only reason Cuban slaveholders stuck to Spain was because they protected the status of slavery.

One of our graduate students, who is Brazilian, explained to me that the "free womb" law by which Brazilians agreed to emancipate their slaves was passed in 1871. So the fate of the Confederacy finished the fate of other slaveholders in the western hemisphere. Can you imagine if they had had any serious toehold on success? It would have been another story entirely in Cuba and in Brazil. At least in Cuba, I think some kind of annexation would have been feasible.

Scott Reynolds Nelson: Audience question: What are some of the biggest misperceptions about home life in the Civil War? There's been a lot written about home life, but we haven't really talked about sassafras tea and all the other ways in which the home front has been talked about. What's the misperception that gets most under your skin about home life in the Confederacy?

Thavolia Glymph: I have one: Sacrifice in the South. Looking through treasury records recently, I began to see ship manifests and bills of lading of goods being shipped down the Mississippi River. Going south were the most expensive wines, hoop skirts, and other luxuries. It was 1863. This is totally in opposition to everything I had heard about sacrifice by Southerners. Here are sugar, wine, and rum moving in an immense contraband trade between North and South. It's not as though the Northerners are unaware. They're making money. They're turning a blind eye. Generals, commanders, civilians in Memphis and Cairo, are all involved in this contraband trade. I found it interesting that not all women had given up their hoop skirts.

Scott Reynolds Nelson: I think of Matamoros and Bermuda; places where all those goods were being smuggled in.

Stephanie McCurry: Help me figure out this misperception. How does the idea persist that the Confederacy was moving toward slave emancipation and somehow they chose independence over slavery? This is the way it's often cast; that at the end of the war, because they needed soldiers, they were willing to enlist black men into the Confederate army. It's an amazing reversal, an epic rise-and-fall story, but it doesn't get cast as a rise-and-fall story. It gets cast as the redemption of the honor of the Confederate nation. If the Confederate government was willing to emancipate slaves (and what they should really be saying is that they were willing to enlist slaves, which is a completely different thing), it means that the Confederacy was choosing independence over slavery. Hence, the war really always was about liberty, states' rights, and national independence.

But in fact the Confederate Constitution had made it impossible on purpose for the federal government ever to emancipate slaves, so when they decided they wanted to enlist them, they had to go begging to the state governments. Virginia was the only ally they had in this, and they couldn't get an emancipation part of that law through.

Still, this story hangs on; that there were significant numbers of black soldiers in the Confederate army, when as far as I know there were only two companies of soldiers, recruited at the very end of the war in Richmond. Most of them were already orderlies and interns working in the hospital in a state of sort of freedom. That myth holds on no matter how much evidence is brought forward to dismiss it, along with the interpretation of that as evidence of Confederate emancipation. There is a gap between popular history and academic history that is so large and never seems to get any smaller.

Eric Foner: What Stephanie is saying, to underline that point: enlisting slaves in the army is not a program for emancipation. Slaves were enlisted in the Continental Army during the American Revolution, but slavery continued. The British enlisted slaves in the 1790s in the West Indies and that did not abolish slavery. Those individuals became free, the black regiments in the West Indies who were fighting the French and the Spanish, but that was in no way connected to a general emancipation. So it is possible to use slave soldiers without in any way committing to ending the institution of slavery.

Stephanie was right; it goes to a larger question of why many people find it hard to accept what Lincoln said: we all know that slavery was the basic cause of the war; to say that is not to say that there was no other cause. There were sources of conflict between East and West, but they didn't lead to an East-West civil war.

There isn't a person alive today who was a slave, and there isn't a person alive today who was a slave-owner during the Civil War, and yet some people hear it as a personal accusation, if they had ancestors who fought for the Confederacy or were connected with the Confederacy. It's hard for them to accept, somehow, that that was the basic cause of the war. Why should it matter what the cause was 150 years ago? It's not a personal insult to you to say that's what was going on.

In 1860 Alexander Stephens, during the secession crisis, wrote a letter to Lincoln about compromise. Stephens was opposed to secession. Lincoln wrote back saying, "I could compromise with you on this and that, but the basic problem is that you think slavery is right and we think slavery is wrong, and I don't see how we can compromise on that." When Stephens was inaugurated as vice president, he gave a famous speech in which he said that slavery was the cornerstone of the Confederacy. Then after the war, Stephens wrote a multivolume history of the war in which he said that the war had nothing to do with slavery. It was all about constitutional interpretation. I don't think seven hundred thousand people go and get killed over constitutional interpretation, frankly.

Slavery as a cause has been pulled out of our understanding of the Civil War. David Blight explained this in *Race and Reunion: The Civil War in American Memory*; to try to put it back in is not an accusation against anybody or any region or people; it's just an attempt to get back to the actual understanding that people had at the time.

J. Matthew Gallman: From the standpoint of the Northern home front, there are many misconceptions, but the most pronounced is the common belief that the Northern army was somehow an army of poor immigrants and hirelings and that it was a rich man's war and a poor man's fight, when in fact the US army during the Civil War was probably the most representative army the United States ever put on the field. By any demographic marker, it was representative among the white soldiers (African-American soldiers are a slightly different demographic) of wealth and class issues—but not marriage—it's largely an unmarried army, which makes perfect sense. In fact the percentage of immigrants who served in the US army during the Civil War was lower than the percentage of immigrants in the country, partly because certain groups of immigrants were opposed to the war, and because aliens were not subject to the draft. People like Martin Scorsese want us to believe that the war was fought by conscripted Irish immigrants who just came off the boat, but that's not true.

Scott Reynolds Nelson: My great grandfather was a conscripted Irish immigrant. (Audience laughter.)

Audience question: When did our present popular conception

of Lincoln as a national hero emerge? We're circling back to Lincoln. How did Lincoln go from being a controversial character to being a hero about whom there are so many biographies ... but only one good one. (Audience laughter.)

Eric Foner: It depends, which is the answer to most history questions. When he died, Lincoln was a hero in the North; in the South it's a little bit different. By the end of the nineteenth century, we have a sort of reconciliation process through the cult of Lincoln and Lee. Jefferson Davis is pushed out; nobody likes Davis, but the cult of Lincoln and Lee emerges in broad popular culture North and South. They represent the best of both societies; Lee is the gentleman, the aristocrat, the thoughtful person; Lincoln is the common man, the emancipator. Both sides can look back with respect to the leader of the other side, in that sense. David Donald wrote in a great essay that everybody has to "get right" with Lincoln. No matter what your position, you have to get Lincoln on your side, retrospectively. This is fine, but it's part of the elision of the African American experience. The cult of Lincoln and Lee leaves no room for Frederick Douglass or the black soldier or many others to be part of the story. It's only recently that the picture of the war has expanded and the cast of characters has expanded. You heard a lot about that today. Our concept of who is a historical actor in the Civil War has expanded way beyond the white soldiers fighting each other—the War of Brothers, as they used to call it.

Scott Reynolds Nelson: That about wraps us up. We've heard a lot about the war outside of Lee and Lincoln. Thank you so much for your time.

Contributors

STEPHEN V. ASH has written or edited ten books and many articles, several of which explore how the people of the South, white and black, experienced Union military invasion and Confederate defeat. An award-winning teacher and scholar, Ash taught at the University of Tennessee until his retirement in 2010.

Ash's books include *When the Yankees Came: Conflict and Chaos in the Occupied South, 1861–1865* (1995); *A Year in the South: 1865* (2004); *Firebrand of Liberty: The Story of Two Black Regiments that Changed the Course of the Civil War* (2008); and *The Black Experience in the Civil War South* (2010). He recently published *A Massacre in Memphis: The Race Riot That Shook the Nation One Year After the Civil War* (2013).

EDWARD L. AYERS is a scholar, teacher, and president of the University of Richmond, author of ten books on the U.S. South, and co-host of BackStory, a nationally syndicated radio show that ties history to the present day.

Ayers is the recipient of numerous honors and awards, including a Bancroft Prize for distinguished writing in American History and the Beveridge Prize for *In the Presence of Mine Enemies, Civil War in the Heart of America* (2004). His book, *The Promise of the New South: Life After Reconstruction* (1992), was a finalist for both the National Book Award and the Pulitzer Prize.

Ayers is co-editor of the "Valley of the Shadow" digital archive and co-primary investigator of "Visualizing Emancipation," a project of the Digital Scholarship Lab of the University of Richmond.

ERIC FONER is a professor of history at Columbia University who has written widely about 19th-century American history and lectured extensively to academic and non-academic audiences.

Foner's books include *Nothing But Freedom: Emancipation and Its Legacy* (1983); *Reconstruction: America's Unfinished Revolution, 1863-1877* (1988), winner of the Bancroft Prize, Parkman Prize, and Los Angeles Times Book Award; and *Who Owns History? Rethinking the Past in a Changing World* (2002). Foner's most recent book, *The Fiery Trial: Abraham Lincoln and American Slavery* (2010), was winner of the Bancroft, Pulitzer, and Lincoln Prizes.

J. MATTHEW GALLMAN is a history professor at University of Florida and author of four books: *Mastering Wartime: A Social History of Philadelphia During the Civil War* (1990); *The North Fights the Civil War: The Home Front* (1994); *Receiving Erin's Children: Philadelphia, Liverpool, and the Irish Famine Migration, 1845–1855* (2000); and *America's Joan of Arc: The Life of Anna Elizabeth Dickinson* (2006). Gallman is currently working on a study of political rhetoric and satire in the North during the Civil War.

THAVOLIA GLYMPH is a professor of history and of African and African American studies at Duke University, where she teaches courses on slavery, the United States South, Emancipation, Reconstruction, and African American women's history.

Glymph is currently completing *Women at War*, a study of women in the Civil War. She is the author of *Out of the House of Bondage: The Transformation of the Plantation Household* (2008) and co-editor of two volumes of *Freedom: A Documentary History of Emancipation, 1861–1867*, a part of the Freedmen and Southern Society Project.

STEPHEN KANTROWITZ is a history professor at the University of Wisconsin-Madison who specializes in the intersections of race, politics, and citizenship in the 19th-century U.S.

Kantrowitz is author of *Ben Tillman and the Reconstruction of White Supremacy* (2000) which was a New York Times Notable Book and won the Ellis W. Hawley Prize from the Organization of American Historians, and *More Than Freedom: Fighting for Black Citizenship in a White Republic, 1829–1889* (2012) He is co-editor of a collection of essays on the history of black Freemasonry, *All Men Free and Brethren,* that was be published in 2013. Kantrowitz's current research includes the impact of Reconstruction on Native American claims to citizenship.

STEPHANIE McCURRY is a history professor at the University of Pennsylvania specializing in American history with a focus on the American South and the Civil War era and the history of women and gender.

Her book, *Masters of Small Worlds: Yeoman Households, Gender Relations and the Political Culture of the South Carolina Low Country* (1995), explored the social and political culture of the state's white majority and their stake in secession. Her book, *Confederate Reckoning: Power and Politics in the Civil War South* (2010), was a finalist for the Pulitzer Prize.

SCOTT REYNOLDS NELSON is a history professor at William & Mary and the author of four books on 19th-century American history. *Steel Drivin' Man*, Nelson's book about the life and legend of John Henry, won four national awards including the National Award for Arts Writing and the Merle Curti Prize for best book in American intellectual history. A young-adult book he co-wrote with Marc Aronson, *Ain't Nothing But a Man*, won seven national awards in 2008.

He also co-wrote, with Carol Sheriff, *A People at War: Civilians and Soldiers in America's Civil War, 1854–1877* (2007). Nelson's latest book is *A Nation of Deadbeats: An Uncommon History of America's Financial Disasters.*

CAROL SHERIFF is a history professor at William & Mary and the author of three books: *The Artificial River: The Erie Canal and the Paradox of Progress, 1817–1862* (1996); *A People at War: Civilians and Soldiers in America's Civil War, 1854–1877* (2007, with co-author Scott Reynolds Nelson); and *A People and A Nation*, a widely used American history textbook that she co-authors with five other scholars.

Sheriff's current research explores the portrayals in children's textbooks of contested historical topics and public responses to such portrayals; she recently published an article in *Civil War History* about state-commissioned Virginia history textbooks.

Further Reading

Further Reading recommendations were contributed by The American Civil War at Home conference participants

Ash, Stephen V. *A Year in the South: 1865: The True Story of Four Ordinary People Who Lived through the Most Tumultuous Twelve Months in American History.* New York: Harper Perennial, 2004.

Ash, Stephen V. *Firebrand of Liberty: The Story of Two Black Regiments that Changed the Course of the Civil War.* New York: W.W. Norton & Company, 2008.

Ash, Stephen V. *When the Yankees Came: Conflict and Chaos in the Occupied South, 1861-1865.* Chapel Hill: University of North Carolina Press, 1999.

Ayers, Edward L. *What Caused the Civil War: Reflections on the South and Southern History.* New York: W.W. Norton & Company, 2006.

Ayers, Edward L. *In the Presence of Mine Enemies: The Civil War in the Heart of America, 1859-1863.* New York: W.W. Norton & Company, 2004.

Ayers, Edward L. *The Promise of the New South: Life After Reconstruction.* Oxford, UK: Oxford University Press, 1993.

Berlin, Ira; Reidy, Joseph P.; and Rowland Leslie S.; eds. *Freedom's Soldiers: The Black Military Experience in the Civil War.* Cambridge, UK: Cambridge University Press, 1998.

Blight, David. *Frederick Douglass' Civil War: Keeping Faith in Jubilee.* Baton Rouge, LA: Louisiana State University Press, 1991.

Blight, David. *Race and Reunion: The Civil War in American Memory.* Cambridge, MA: Belknap Press, 2002.

Bynum, Victoria E. *Unruly Women: The Politics of Social and Sexual Control in the Old South.* Chapel Hill: University of North Carolina Press, 1992.

Chang, Kornel. *Pacific Connections: The Making of the U.S.-Canadian Borderlands.* Berkeley, CA: University of California Press: 2012.

Downs, Jim. *Sick from Freedom: African-American Illness and Suffering during the Civil*

War and Reconstruction New York: Oxford University Press, 2012.

Escott, Paul D. *"What Shall We Do with the Negro?" Lincoln, White Racism, and Civil War America*. Charlottesville: University of Virginia Press, 2009.

Fahs, Alice. *The Imagined Civil War Popular Literature of the North and South, 1861-1865*. Chapel Hill: University of North Carolina Press, 2000.

Faust, Drew Gilpin. *Creation of Confederate Nationalism Ideology and Identity in the Civil War South*. Baton Rouge, LA: Louisiana State University Press, 1990.

Faust, Drew Gilpin. *Mothers of Invention: Women of the Slaveholding South in the Civil War*. Chapel Hill: University of North Carolina Press, 2004.

Foner, Eric. *The Fiery Trial: Abraham Lincoln and American Slavery*. New York: W.W. Norton & Company, 2010.

Foner, Eric. *Nothing But Freedom: Emancipation and its Legacy*. Baton Rouge, LA: Louisiana State University Press, 2007.

Foner, Eric. *Reconstruction: America's Unfinished Revolution, 1863-1877*. New York: HarperCollins, 1988.

Foner, Eric. *The Story of American Freedom* New York: W. W. Norton and Co, 1998.

Gallagher, Gary. *The Union War*. Cambridge, MA: Harvard University Press, 2011.

Gallman, James M. *The North Fights the Civil War: The Home Front*. Chicago: Ivan R. Dee, 1994.

Gallman, James M. *Northerners at War: Reflections on the Civil War Home Front (Civil War in the North)*. Kent, OH: Kent State University Press, 2010.

Gallman, James M. *The Civil War Chronicle*. Old Saybrook, CT: Konecky & Konecky, 2010.

Glymph, Thavolia. *Out of the House of Bondage: The Transformation of the Plantation Household*. Cambridge, UK: Cambridge University Press, 2008.

Hahn, Steven. *A Nation Under Our Feet: Black Political Struggles in the Rural South from Slavery to the Great Migration*. Cambridge, MA: Belknap Press of Harvard University Press, 2005.

Hahn, Steven. *The Political Worlds of Slavery and Freedom*. Cambridge, MA: Harvard University Press, 2009.

Harris, Leslie. *In the Shadow of Slavery: African Americans in New York City, 1626-1863*. Chicago, IL: University of Chicago Press, 2003.

Hinks, Peter P.; and Kantrowitz, Stephen; eds. *All Men Free and Brethren: Essays on the History of African American Freemasonry* Ithaca, NY: Cornell University Press, 2013.

Hinks, Peter P. *To Awaken My Afflicted Brethren: David Walker and the Problem of Antebellum Slave Resistance.* University Park, PA: Penn State University Press, 2006.

Kantrowitz, Stephen. *More Than Freedom: Fighting for Black Citizenship in a White Republic, 1829-1889.* London, UK: Penguin Books, 2012.

Kantrowitz, Stephen. *Ben Tillman and the Reconstruction of White Supremacy* Chapel Hill: UNC Press, 2000.

Litwack, Leon. *Been in the Storm So Long: The Aftermath of Slavery* New York: Vintage Books, 1980.

McCurry, Stephanie. *Confederate Reckoning: Power and Politics in the Civil War South.* Cambridge, MA: Harvard University Press, 2010.

McCurry, Stephanie. *Masters of Small Worlds: Yeoman Households, Gender Relations, and the Political Culture of the Antebellum South Carolina Low Country.* Oxford, UK: Oxford University Press, 1995.

Neely, Mark E. *Lincoln and the Triumph of the Nation: Constitutional Conflict in the American Civil War.* Chapel Hill: University of North Carolina Press, 2011.

Nelson, Scott R.; and Sheriff, Carol. *A People at War: Civilians and Soldiers in America's Civil War.* New York: Oxford University Press, USA, 2007.

Paddison, Joshua. *American Heathens: Religion, Race, and Reconstruction in California.* San Marino, CA: Huntington Library Press, 2012.

Robinson, Armstead L. *Bitter Fruits of Bondage: The Demise of Slavery and the Collapse of the Confederacy, 1861-1865.* Charlottesville: University of Virginia Press, 2005.

Roediger, David; and Esch, Elizabeth. *The Production of Difference: Race and the Management of Labor in U.S. History.* New York: Oxford University Press, USA, 2012.

Sandow, Robert. *Deserter Country: Civil War Opposition in the Pennsylvania Appalachians.* Bronx, NY: Fordham University Press, 2011.

Smith, Stacey L. *Freedom's Frontier: California and the Struggle over Unfree Labor, Emancipation, and Reconstruction.* Chapel Hill: University of North Carolina Press, 2013.

Thomas, Emory M. *The Confederacy as a Revolutionary Experience.* Columbia, SC: University of South Carolina Press. 1992.

Witt, John Fabian. *Lincoln's Code: The Laws of War in American History.* New York: Free Press, 2012

Index

36-30 Line, 95
54th Regiment Massachusetts Volunteer Infantry, 32, 33

A Few Words in Behalf of the Loyal Women of the United States (Anonymous), 68
abolitionism, x, xii, xiv, 2-4, 6-7, 8, 9, 12, 25, 29, 31, 33, 36, 79, 87
activism, black Northern, xii, 27, 29, 31-32, 33, 34; civil rights, 1; white Northern, 29, 31, 74-75, 79; white Southern, 51, 76-77
Alabama, 9
Alexandria, Va., 41, 84
American Revolution, 6, 98
Andersonville Prison, 89
Antietam, Md., battle of, 9
Apache Tribe, 95
Appeal to the Coloured Citizens (Walker), 29
Appomattox, Va., xi, 17, 93
Arizona, 95, 96
Arthur's Home Magazine, 66
Arthur, Timothy Shay, 66
Ash, Stephen V., xiii, 54-61, 72-73, 75, 77, 79, 81, 83, 86
Asian Americans, 85
Ayers, Ed, xi, 15-20, 36, 38. 39-40, 41-43, 44, 45-46, 78; *Visualizing Emancipation*, xi, 15, 16, 17, 38, 44

Beersheba Springs, Tn., xiii, 58, 75
Belvidere Baptist Church, 52
Bermuda, 97

Black Laws of Illinois, 4
Blight, David, 99
border slave states, 7, 9, 12, 46, 94
Boston, Mass., xii, 29-31, 32, 33, 36, 69
Brazil, 94
Bread Riots, Southern, 51-52
Brown, John, 6, 36
Brown, William Wells, 33
Burns, Anthony, 29, 36

Cairo, Ill., 97
California, 85, 94
Cameron Plantation, 37
Canada, 64
Chase, Salmon P., 9, 88
Cherokee Tribe, 92, 93, 94
Chicago Tribune, 67, 69
Chickasaw Tribe, 92
Chihuahua, Mexico, 95
Choctaw Tribe, 92
Christianity, 28, 68-69
Clay, Henry, 5-6, 28
Coles, Edward, 5
colonization of African Americans, x, xii, 5, 7, 9, 10, 11, 12, 22, 28, 29; of African Americans in Africa, x, 5, 7; of African Americans in the Caribbean, x, 5; of African Americans in Central America, 5; Lincoln's support of, x, xii, 5, 7, 9, 10, 11, 12, 22, 28, 33
Comanche Tribe, 95
Concordia Parish, La., 21

Confederate army, xi, 18, 23, 25, 35, 39, 41, 42, 44-46, 50, 52, 56, 57, 60, 72, 76-77, 92, 95; black enlistment in, 97-98; seizure/destruction of property by, 41, 50, 72, 78; use of African Americans for labor by, 7, 19, 42, 44; white enlistment in, xii-xiii, 50, 76, 78

Confederate Reckoning (McCurry), xii, 40

conscription, 17, 39, 74; Confederate, 39, 44, 50, 52, 72; Union, 41-42, 45, 63-64, 66-67, 74, 99

Constitution, Confederate, 74, 97

Constitution, United States, x, 2, 3-4, 6, 36, 80

contraband, 83; African Americans as, 24, 45; camps, 41; Union policy toward, xi, 24, 45. *See also*: refugee, African Americans as.

Continental Army, 98

Copperheads, xiii, 62

Cotton is King Speech, 96

Creek Tribe, 92, 93

Crittenden Resolutions, 95

Cuba, 85, 94, 96

Cuffe, Paul, 7

CS War Department, 74

Davis Bend, 26

Davis, Emily, 87

Davis, Jefferson, 37, 50, 90, 100

Declaration of Independence, 2, 4, 9, 28, 49

Delaware, 7

DeLay, Brian, 95

Delhi, LA, 21

Democratic Party, 3, 4, 62, 92

Donald, David, 100

Douglas, Stephen A., 4

Douglass, Frederick, 32, 46, 88, 100

Downs, Greg, 84

Dred Scott decision, 88

DuBois, W.E.B., 41, 46

Dyer Compendium, 15

Egyptian army, 85

Ely, Melvin Patrick, ix

emancipation, x-xi, xii, xiv, 1-2, 5-13, 15-17, 19-20, 21, 22, 26, 27, 34, 44, 45-46, 49, 54, 61, 75-76, 87, 88, 93, 96-98; compensation of slaveholders for, x, 6, 7, 8, 10-12, 46-47

Emancipation Proclamation, x, xi, 1, 9-12, 13, 14, 19, 22, 26, 27, 32, 34, 38, 42, 44, 86-88

enlistment, 6, 58, 62, 67; of African Americans in the Union Army, x-xi, 2, 6, 10-11, 22, 32, 33, 78; of African Americans in the Confederate army, 97-98; of white Northerners in the Union army, x, xiii, 8, 63, 67; of white Southerners in the Union army, xiii, 57; of whites in the Confederate army, xii-xiii, 50, 76

Esch, Elizabeth, 85; *Production of Difference*, 85

Faulkner, William, 37

Fiery Trial, The (Foner), x, 2

First Confiscation Act, 7, 26, 44

Florida, 56, 96

Foner, Eric, x-xi, xii, 1-14, 79, 86-87, 91-92, 93, 96, 98-99, 100; *The Fiery Trial*, x, 2

Fortress Monroe, 17

Fort Sumter, 13, 46. 88, 93

Fort Wagner, 35

Forten, Charlotte, 23

Fourteenth Amendment, 80

Frank Leslie's Budget of Fun, 64

Freedmen's Bureau, 24, 41, 43, 83

Freedmen's Department, 24, 43

Freedom's Frontier (Smith), 85

French, Virginia, 58

Fugitive Slave Act, 36, 38

Gallman, J. Matthew, xiii, 62-70, 73, 74, 77, 79-80, 81, 84-85, 87, 93-94, 99

Garrison, William Lloyd, 3, 6, 29

General Order 100 (Lieber Code), 26

Georgia, 72

Gettysburg Address, 4

Gettysburg, Pa., 77; battle of, 35, 38, 43

Gilded Age, 91

Glymph, Thavolia, xi, 21-26, 37, 38, 40-41, 43, 44-45, 46, 47, 78, 83, 85, 88, 90-91, 94, 96-97

Goodrich's Landing, La., 25
Great Britain, support of the Confederacy by, x, 8
greenback, ix
Greenback Party, 92

Haiti, 87-88; revolution in, 6
Hammond, James Henry, 96
Hampton, Va., xi, 19, 41
Harper's New Monthly Magazine, 64
Hawaii, 85
Hilton Head, S.C., 41, 78
Howell, William, vii-viii
How a Free People Conduct a Long War (Stillé), 66
Huntington, F.D., 69

Jackson, Andrew, 96
Jackson, Mary, 52
Jacobs, Harriet, 23
James River, 55
Jefferson, Thomas, 5-6
Johnson, Andrew, xiii, 9, 60, 61
Johnson, Walter, 95

Kansas, 43, 93
Kantrowitz, Stephen, xii, 27-34, 35-36, 38, 42, 45, 46, 47, 82, 85, 87-88, 90, 92-93, 95, 96
Kentucky, 3, 7, 9, 36, 45

Lake Providence, 21
Lee, Robert E., 9, 74, 100
Lieber Code, 26, 84
Lincoln, Abraham, x-xi, xii, xiv, 1-14, 15, 16, 19, 22, 28, 33, 34, 46-47, 62, 84, 87, 93, 95, 98-100
Litwack, Leon, 83
Louisiana, 9, 12, 17, 21, 33, 59, 88
Lowell, Mass., 92
Lumpkin's Jail, 36

Madison, James, 7
Maryland, 7, 9, 12
Massasoit Guard, 32
Matamoros, 97
McClellan, George, 9, 12, 46

McCurry, Stephanie, xii-xiii, 40, 48-53, 71-72, 73-74, 75, 76-79, 80-81, 82-83, 86, 89-90, 94-95, 96, 97-98; *Confederate Reckoning*, xii, 40
Memphis, Tenn., 84, 86, 97; race riot in, 86
Mexico, 94, 95, 96
Milliken's Bend, 21
Militia Act, 44
Mississippi, 9, 24, 39, 41, 57, 59, 72, 78, 90
Mississippi River, 17, 38, 97
Missouri, 7, 12, 17
Mobile, Al., xiii, 51, 52, 56
Mobile Bay, 17
Morris, Robert, 31-33

Nashville, Tn., xiii, 56, 59
Nasmith, Samuel J., 25
Native Americans, 82-83, 85, 92-95
Negro Fort, 96
Nelson, Scott, ix-xiv, 35, 36-37, 38-39, 40, 41, 43, 44, 46, 82, 84, 86, 89, 90, 91, 92, 96, 97, 99-100; *People at War, A*, 84
Nesbit, Scott, xi
New Mexico, 95, 96
New Orleans, La., xiii, 56, 96
New York, state of, 35
New York City, N.Y., 92; draft riot in, 74-75
Northerners, xiii, 3, 8, 37, 41, 55-56, 59-60, 62-70, 73, 79, 97; free black, xii, 27-34, 36, 90; white, x, xiv, 22. *See also* women: Northern white.
North Carolina, 29, 36, 57, 59, 72, 86, 90

Office of the United Nations High Commmissioner for Refugees (UNHCR), the, 26
Official Records of the War of the Rebellion, 15
Ohio, 90
Ohio River, 3
Oklahoma, 93
Oregon, 85, 94

Peake, Mary, 23
Pensacola, Fla., 56
People at War, A (Nelson and Sheriff), 84
Peoria, Il., Lincoln's speech in, 4

Philadelphia, Pa., 87, 94
Philadelphia Historical Society, 87
Philippines, the, 85
Phillips, Wendell, 6
Pointe Couppe Parish, La., 61
poke salad, ix, xiii
Port Lookout, 89
Preliminary Emancipation Proclamation, 9-11, 47
Production of Difference, The (Roediger and Esch), 85

Radical Republicans, 2, 7, 12
railroad, 17, 51, 91
Readjusters, 92
Reconstruction, 12, 19, 61, 79, 83-84
Redpath, James, 87
refugee, African Americans as, xi-xii, 23-26, 36-38, 41, 43, 83; African Americans escaping to Union lines, x, xi, xiv, 1, 8, 16-17, 22-26, 37, 44; camps, 17, 23, 24, 25, 26, 41, 43; white Confederate, xi, 39, 41, 56, 78, 94; white southern Union, xi, 26, 56
Republican Party, 2, 5, 6, 7, 11, 12, 92
Revels, Hiram, 90
Richmond, Va., ix, 18, 19, 36, 39, 42, 46, 51-52, 55, 98
Roediger, David, 85; *Production of Difference*, 85
Ruffin, Edmund, 39, 46

San Francisco, Ca., 85
Sand Creek Massacre, 94
Savannah, Ga., xiii, 45, 56, 60
secession, xi, xii, xiii, 6, 16, 36, 40, 45-46, 48-49, 72, 79, 88, 90, 93, 94, 98
Second Confiscation Act, 8, 10, 26, 44
Seddon, James, 37
Seminole Tribe, 92
Scorsese, Martin, 99
Shaw, Robert Gould, 33
Sheriff, Carol, ix, 71, 73, 74, 75, 77, 79, 84; *People at War, A*, 84
Sherman, William Tecumseh, 43, 44-45
Shiloh, Battle of, 37
shoddy, ix, xiii, 64

slave-owners. *See* Southerners, white: slaveholding.
Slave Power conspiracy, 31
slavery, ix-xii, xiv, 1-14, 15-19, 21-26, 27, 28-29, 31, 33, 35-36, 37, 38, 39-41, 42, 43, 45-47, 48-50, 53, 57, 59, 72, 76, 77, 78, 80, 82, 88, 89, 95, 96, 97, 98-99; constitutional protection of, x, 3-4, 6
Smith, Margaret, 86
Smith, Stacy, 85; *Freedom's Frontier*, 85
Sonora, Mexico, 95
South Carolina, 9, 36, 38-39, 40, 60, 77, 78, 91
South Carolina Declaration of Immediate Causes, 36
Southerners, white, xi, xiii, 19, 32, 38, 46, 48, 56, 89, 90: non-slaveholding, xiii, 49, 59, 71, 76-77, 80; poor, xiii, xiv, 50, 53, 54-61, 71, 73, 75, 76, 79, 91; slaveholding, x, xiii, 6, 7, 8, 10, 12, 22, 24, 25, 26, 28, 29, 31, 39, 40-41, 45, 46, 47, 48-50, 54, 57, 59, 76-77, 78, 87, 93, 95; women. *See* women, white Southern.
Spain, 95, 96
Speed, Joshua, 3
Spotsylvania County, Va., 60
St. Louis, Mo., 3
Stephens, Alexander, 94, 98-99
Stillé, Charles, 66; *How a Free People Conduct a Long War*, 66
suffrage, African-American, 12, 33-34, 79; women's, 79

tar heel, ix
Taylor, Susie King, 23
Tennessee, xiii, 9, 36, 55, 57, 58, 59, 72, 77, 84; Unionists in, 57, 72
Tennessee River, 17
Texas, 38-39, 77, 78, 94
Thirteenth Amendment, xi, 1, 7, 12, 16, 19
Tierra del Fuego, 96
Troy, N.Y., 92
Truth, Sojourner, 23
Tubman, Harriet, 23
Tyler, John, 40

Union Army, x, xi, xiii, 8, 10, 11, 15, 16, 17, 18, 19, 22-24, 35, 36-37, 38, 41-42, 43, 44-46, 53, 54, 55, 56, 60, 77-78, 84, 90, 92-93, 94, 95, 99; African American assistance of, 18, 22, 37, 38, 45; African American enlistment in, x, 2, 10, 22, 32, 33, 78; seizure/destruction of property by, 17, 41, 42, 52, 78; white Northern enlistment in, x, xiii, 8, 64; white Southern enlistment in, xiii, 57

University of Richmond, xi, 15

US Congress, ix, 8, 10, 12, 24, 26, 61, 86, 90

US Treasury Department, 24, 41, 43

US War Department, 33, 43

Virginia, xi, 9, 15, 16, 17, 18, 19, 36, 39, 43, 46, 49, 55, 56, 57, 59, 60, 74, 77, 84, 90, 92, 94, 97

Visualizing Emancipation (Ayers, Nesbit), xi, 15 16, 17, 38, 44

Walker, David, 29; *Appeal to the Coloured Citizens, 29*

Walker, J.G., 21

Washington, D.C., 7, 8, 13, 19

Washington, state of, 85, 94

Western Sanitary Commission, 25

Whig Party, 28

Whittenburg, James, ix

Williamsburg, Va., 17, 18

Winchester, Va., 18

women, 18, 23, 41, 44, 79, 91, 97; African-American, xi, xii, xiv, 3, 11, 18, 21, 21-26, 37, 38, 43-45, 87, 88; white Southern, xiii, 23, 25, 26, 49-53, 54, 58, 59, 68, 71-72, 75, 76-77, 78, 80-81, 86, 89, 91; white Northern, 23, 25, 29, 56, 63, 67-68, 74-75, 79-80

World War II, 83

BOOKS FROM THE SIGNATURE CONFERENCE SERIES

VOLUME ONE

America on the Eve of the Civil War, from the 2009 conference at the University of Richmond. Edited by Edward L. Ayers and Carolyn Martin.

VOLUME TWO

Race, Slavery and the Civil War: The Tough Stuff of American History and Memory, from the 2010 Signature Conference at Norfolk State University. Edited by James O. Horton and Amanda Kleintop.

VOLUME THREE

Military Strategy in the American Civil War, from the 2011 Signature Conference at Virginia Tech. Edited by James I. Robertson, Jr.

VOLUME FOUR

Leadership and Generalship in the Civil War, from the 2012 Signature Conference at Virginia Military Institute. Edited by John W. Knapp.

VOLUME FIVE

The American Civil War at Home, from the 2013 Signature Conference at the College of William & Mary. Edited by Scott Reynolds Nelson and Carol Sheriff.

AVAILABLE ON DVD

Virginia in the Civil War: A Sesquicentennial Remembrance, an Emmy-nominated video documentary from Executive Producer James I. Robertson, Jr.

The Signature Conference series is a project of the Virginia Sesquicentennial of the American Civil War Commission.

WWW.VIRGINIACIVILWAR.ORG/MARKETPLACE